A

MW01042812

"David Wells is advisir   ̣
is Possible, why and how to develop a wealth strategy for all five
of ours and our families' capitals: spiritual, social, intellectual,
human and financial. He succeeds profoundly in teaching us
how to understand each capital and its evolution toward its
dynamic preservation and then to ours' and our families' happiness as a result."

- James (Jay) E. Hughes, Jr.

Author of *Family Wealth: Keeping it in the Family* and *Family: The
Compact Among Generations* and co-author of *The Cycle of the Gift, The
Voice of the Rising Generation, Complete Family Wealth* and *Family Trusts*

"David Wells has written a best-in-class teaching book on the
meaning and practice of wealth. It provides not only a com-
pendium of knowledge about the trends and social-psychology
of wealth, but also a wise understanding about how to grow,
and use wealth for self, heirs, and philanthropy. It is a formative book to be read by and with our adult children."

- Paul G. Schervish

Professor Emeritus and Founding Director of the Center
on Wealth and Philanthropy at Boston College

"In *When Anything Is Possible*, David C. Wells, Jr. identifies what it means to be truly wealthy – as opposed to merely having a lot of money. He asks the core questions: "Why do we want the things we want?" "What is our wealth really for?" Wealthy families want to know how to use their wealth productively, improving both the happiness of their own families and also the wellbeing of the society that allowed them to become wealthy in the first place. These are complex issues, but Wells lays out the key strategies families need to follow. Wealthy families who want their grandchildren to be happy and productive citizens should keep this book close to hand."

– Gregory Curtis

Founder, Greycourt & Co., Inc. and author of *Family Capital*

"People often view the task of managing wealth as largely an investment exercise. David C. Wells, Jr.'s When Anything is Possible shows that it is much, much more. Read this book to [This book will] open your eyes about all of the components of wealth management strategy you might currently be missing, and then get started addressing the gaps with Wells' framework and concise and curated list of resources. Wells also hits the nail on the head with his assertion that any truly successful wealth management strategy begins with looking within and answering for yourself a number of questions, starting with "Why?" If you think there is nothing left to do on the wealth management front in your situation, read this book and prepare to be surprised."

– Coventry Edwards-Pitt

CFA, CFP®, author of Raised Healthy, Wealthy & Wise and
Chief Wealth Advisory Officer, Ballentine Partners, LLC"

"*When Anything is Possible* surveys the increasingly broad landscape where psychology and wealth intersect. David Wells touches on everything from wealth adjustment, identity, transition, and stereotyping to behavioral finance and investment psychology. If you are psychologically minded yet rationally motivated, this is your book."

– James Grubman PhD
author of *Strangers in Paradise: How Families Adapt to Wealth Across Generation*

"David Wells's *When Anything Is Possible* is an impressive debut. Taking cues from lions in the wealth industry like Jay Hughes and marrying them to modern thinkers like Daniel Kahneman within the framework of his own experience, David has authored an insightful guidebook for the wealthy. This is not a "Get Rich, Stay Rich" book. *When Anything is Possible* tackles the important problem of helping people define the role of wealth in their lives. Then, it provides the tools to help those people move forward in an organized way and build lives of purpose. This is now a permanent part of my reading list for clients and people in the wealth industry."

- Frazer Rice
Regional Director, Pendleton Square Trust Company,
Author and Host of "Wealth, Actually"

"David has written a very useful, practical and accessible book about the personal dynamics of wealth. Rather than a book about trusts, tax and financial strategies this is about the personal side of wealth. It helps the family step back and look at the purpose behind their wealth, what it means to them, and the impact they want to see in their lives. The book is clear and full of practical activities and questions to answer, that guide you on your own personal and family wealth journey."

- Dennis T. Jaffe, PhD

Wise Counsel Research, author of *Borrowed from your Grandchildren: The Evolution of 100-Year Family Enterprises*

"Ideally all books on wealth would be as accessible as Wells' contribution to the field. *When Anything is Possible - Wealth and the Art of Strategic Living* gives people the guidance they need to face the nearly limitless set of choices they encounter when coming into wealth; and does so in a way that acknowledges who they are beyond just their financial resources."

- Sharna Goldseker

Founder & Vice President, 21/64. Co-Author, *Generation Impact: How Next Gen Donors Are Revolutionizing Giving*

"*When Anything is Possible* lays out the framework required to harness financial capital into a life-enhancing force. David Wells truly understands the human side of wealth — with all of its promise and baggage — and has leveraged his experience, empathy and creativity to curate both tested and innovative ideas into a roadmap that will prove valuable to individuals at any level of financial success."

- Jim Coutré

family office and philanthropy professional

WHEN

ANYTHING IS

POSSIBLE

WHEN
ANYTHING IS
POSSIBLE

WEALTH AND THE ART OF STRATEGIC LIVING

DAVID C. WELLS, JR.

When Anything is Possible

ISBN: 978-1-7356813-0-6

Library of Congress Control Number: 2020917711

First paperback edition published October 2020

Book design by G Sharp Design, LLC.
www.gsharpmajor.com

Special thanks to Mary Ann McGuigan for her indefatigable efforts in editing the manuscript.

For my wife, Meredith,
who survived a thousand late night conversations
as these ideas came to life.

CONTENTS

PREFACE

"Of all the classes, the wealthy are the most noticed and the least studied."

—JOHN KENNETH GALBRAITH

———

T he subject of finance has generated a broad spectrum of books. I've read more than 200 of them—and counting.[1] Finance books fall into three major categories. First, there are the *I have a problem and need help* books. Think Dave Ramsey. Dave and others do a great job of deconstructing what comes down to a spending issue along with a lack of financial education to provide concrete steps for a path forward.

Then there are the *I have a little money and want more of it* (or introduction to investing) books. At best, these books amount to pop psychology meets money, designed for the lay reader and providing some rough direction about how

———

1 To see my favorites, organized by topic, visit www.davidcwellsjr.com/readinglist

to begin investing/saving for retirement; at worst, they're long on hyperbole and short on specifics.

Finally, there are textbook like deep-dives on specific financial topics—investing, real estate, etc.—but they're generally inaccessible for the average reader or the non-financial professional, unless they provide a lot of additional background.

Whether the topic is accumulation of wealth or the management of it, it's been covered at some length. Many of them have value. In fact, some are arguably must-reads for a prudent approach to one's financial affairs. *When Anything Is Possible* offers something quite different from any other book. Consider it a guide. It's about helping you draft your financial blueprints.

I view myself as a strategist, investor, and entrepreneur; my work has placed me in all three of those roles. I began my professional career spending almost seven years on Wall Street as a research analyst; then came four years as a portfolio manager at a hedge fund I co-founded in 2012. I spent eleven years in deep analysis, predominately of consumer companies, covering everything from low-income retail to golf equipment, to recreational vehicles, and finally the media business. As an analyst and portfolio manager, I focused on developing a comprehensive understanding of how these businesses structured themselves, how they positioned their strategies in the marketplace, and how and why consumers chose to purchase their goods and services to enhance their lives.

Over the course of my career, I've spent hundreds of hours with company CEOs and CFOs and some of the world's smartest investors and I've watched how they analyze and guide their businesses. I was able to start several businesses, review pitchbooks for hundreds of private equity and hedge funds, and serve on advisory boards for several nonprofit organizations.

As my career on Wall Street developed, it took a surprising turn when I discovered the family office world and was introduced to the unique challenges that families of significant means face as they seek to steward their considerable wealth through the generations.

Writing the Book I Needed for Myself

In many ways, this book is a response to my own need for this resource and to the thousands of similar questions I've heard from clients who wrestle with these issues. How each of us integrates our own experiences with the presence or absence of wealth is a key component of our happiness.

In 2001, I finished high school and matriculated to Wake Forest University, in Winston-Salem, NC. I grew up in what I would now consider a small town, Roanoke, VA. Roanoke, depending on how you define it and how geographically generous you are, has somewhere around 250,000 residents. It's an altogether average American town. We had movie theaters, malls, and most chain restaurants, but not a Nordstrom.

As the son of a local physician, my upbringing would be considered upper middle class, which means we were probably among the top 10 percent of income but certainly not the 0.1 percent. One wonderful aspect of growing up in this environment was an almost complete absence of any effort to "keep up with the Joneses." I went to a normal high school with a group of normal middle-class folks. Looking back on it now, I'm struck that my upper-middle-class status, of which I was largely ignorant, was probably very clear to my classmates. Oh, well, such is the blissful naiveté of youth.

So when I arrived at Wake's campus, I assumed it would be filled with people like me. Perhaps to an extent it was, but a sizable portion of the student body was from the true upper class of society. The sons and daughters of Fortune 500 CEOs, owners of sizable family businesses, and even a member of the Walton family made us kids from normal hardworking professionals, doctors, lawyers, and the like look relatively impoverished.

As an eighteen-year-old, I was immediately struck—dumbfounded, in fact—by some of my new classmates: the friend whose family owned a beautiful vacation house in Beaver Creek, the buddy whose family's construction company had just finished building the new corporate headquarters for one of the hottest tech companies in the country. After the culture shock subsided, I made friends with a group of people whose upbringing mostly looked pretty

WHEN ANYTHING IS POSSIBLE

close to my own. I graduated and moved to Charlotte, NC, and took a job in consulting.

Starting a new job was stressful financially. I started adulthood with about $1,000 I'd saved from summer jobs, lived in a reasonably priced apartment, and cooked a lot of my own meals. Within a few short months, I'd saved a little extra money and could breathe a little easier. As I got older, I always kept a list of things that would be nice to own one day, when I had money and a real job. (I keep a similar list today).

I realized fairly quickly, I could have almost anything I wanted, even at college graduate starting salaries; I just couldn't have everything. This was a major revelation for me. I was able to afford many things that I'd always considered necessities and many things that were clearly *wants*.

As my career has progressed and salaries have increased, this reality has remained true: the ability to have anything but not everything. And I discovered as I interacted with hundreds of millionaires and billionaires, it's true for them too. We're not able to have everything we want all the time. Our desires don't work like that. They always seem to rise to include the unattainable. And what we want in life isn't always quantifiable or able to be purchased. The fact is we must each wrestle with the question of what we want from our lives and why. This book is my attempt to help people answer that question.

As Francis Bacon tells us, "Money is a great servant but a bad master." So the core questions we must wrestle with are *Why do we want the things we want? And what is the purpose behind the wealth we have or are seeking to create?*

In many ways, the book is the repayment of a debt of gratitude to an extraordinary gentleman I've been privileged to spend time with. For the vast majority of Americans, the name James (Jay) Hughes likely means very little. But to a select group of families of substantial means, along with their trusted advisors, Jay is the guru's guru.

A trusted advisor to many families, Jay has made a significant contribution to the literature regarding families and wealth. After spending the entirety of his career working with families to create trusts and other vehicles to perpetuate a family's wealth, Jay's career took a fortuitous turn when he began exploring the effects of inheriting great wealth, asking the "victims of a prior generation's largess" whether they felt this was in fact a good thing. Astonishingly, Jay found that the vast majority of beneficiaries of a trust (more than 80 percent) found the trust had a negative impact in their lives.

This finding prompted Jay to begin what I can only characterize as significant soul searching as he looked for a path forward for his life's work. Arguably, this path forward was marked by his the publication of his book *Family Wealth: Keeping It in the Family* in 2004. *Family Wealth* became the go-to text for families who are seriously and thoughtfully considering what the propagation of wealth looks like in a multigenerational context. In it, Jay makes clear that families who neglect spiritual (values), social (societal), human, and intellectual capital of their family and instead focus only on the family's financial wherewithal are destined to experience the oft-repeated and globally known curse of *shirtsleeves to shirtsleeves* in three generations—that is, the loss of wealth by the third generation.

In a larger sense, I would argue that Jay's even more foundational contribution to the discourse around wealth has been to ask a delightfully simple question: why?

As someone classically educated in high school and a student of philosophy and business at university, *why* is perhaps my favorite question. *Whyness* is perhaps a bit more in vogue these days, thanks to British/American author Simon Sinek's excellent TED Talk and book *Start with Why*.

But the entirety of the financial-advice industry—whether in books, blogs, or videos—is structured around technique: *how* to go from lacking wealth to attaining it. In that approach, almost no consideration is given to the *why* behind the wealth and what to do with the wealth once it's attained.

Even today, at my own firm, working with families to articulate the structure and strategy to stay invested together over time, far too many clients have a hard time articulating how and why they do what they do with their financial wealth. Arguably, this is the reason I found Hughes's book so delightful. It was as if this desire/quest for the why behind wealth had begun to find its expression in the mind of Mr. Hughes. *Family Wealth* stands largely alone in the world of books on personal finance.

INTRODUCTION

"The most unhappy person in town is the former CEO who sold his company for $50 million, eighteen months ago."

—LONG-TIME FINANCIAL ADVISOR

———

The rise of income inequality in the world, especially in the United States, has become a front-burner issue. You can scarcely open a newspaper today without a story on it, along with a whole host of proposals about how to fix the problem. The issue is of great importance and has implications for our politics and, more broadly, for how society is constituted. Still, the American dream and our strong belief in meritocracy keep our culture rife with books and resources on *how to make it big*.

Although we're quick to talk about wealth as an abstract concept, talking about wealth at a personal level remains challenging at best and taboo at worst. But wealth for all of us is intimately connected with our own human story. Consider the following examples:

→ After selling his company to a private equity firm, a CEO asks us to come meet with him. He had made $50 million and was looking for someone to manage a conservative bond portfolio worth $25 million. He ultimately decides to keep the money in cash because his house was paid off and his standard of living so low that he could not foresee how he would ever spend his windfall.

→ Three siblings inherit a family company, with each having a share worth almost $100 million. Their father had told them never to depend on the company generating any wealth for them, so they live on only $200,000 a year—less than 1 percent of their net worth.

→ A thirty-seven-year-old entrepreneur sells her company and makes $5 million. She has enough money to do anything she wants but not enough to do nothing if she wants to be able to live the lifestyle she desires as she ages. How should she contemplate finding a new job? Start another company? Invest the proceeds?

Consider the following statistics:

→ Studies show lottery winners are no happier after their win than they were before.

→ Eighty percent of trust beneficiaries do not view their trust as a beneficial presence in their life.

→ Roy Williams and Vic Presser, in the research that led to their book *Preparing Heirs*, note that 70 percent of estate plans fall apart after the estate owner's death.

We know that wealth inequality is increasing, and from the ubiquity of social media, we're able to see its effects on consumption in the lives of celebrities (for example, *Keeping up with the Kardashians*) or in the lives of our friends and acquaintances. Rarely, however, are the beneficiaries of this newfound wealth asked how they're doing. How are they adapting to this newly acquired financial largess?

Surprisingly, the answer is *not particularly well.* There have been a couple studies over the last few years that have shown that those who are the most well off still feel highly insecure financially. This is not to bemoan the plight of the well-to-do. Nor is it about casting blame or shame on those who've been the net beneficiaries of this societal shift. As the Teacher of Ecclesiastes remarks, "The race is not to the swift, nor yet riches to men of understanding, nor yet favor to men of skill, but time and chance happens to them all." There truly are an infinite number of paths that end with someone becoming wealthy.

Wealth leaves no facet of life untouched; therefore, how we think and feel about our wealth is intimately tied to how we think and feel about our lives. When the wealthy feel intimidated by the implications of their wealth, insecure in its provision, or uncertain about how to move forward with their lives, they live lives that are not what they could be.

When this happens, we all suffer—both rich and poor. When a whole segment of society remains adrift about how to move forward, society as a whole suffers because it misses out on the creative dynamism that such folks bring to their endeavors. Our capital markets suffer as new ventures go unfunded. And, of course, the nonprofits that depend on charitable dollars are limited as to how high their ambitions for change can reach.

But like the proverbial dog who catches the bus he has worked so hard to chase, once we attain the status of *rich*—however we may define it—we may have given very little thought to what that means and what we want to do with the wealth we've attained. Instead of enjoying the wealth and the opportunities it brings, we become plagued by uncertainty and fear, whether because we're busy comparing our lifestyle to how others define a rich life or because we're desperately trying to avoid raising entitled *trust fund brats*.

What's needed is a shift in mindset, a shift away from the tactics of making wealth to the key strategic considerations behind using wealth well. This book is designed to be a guide, to help articulate what such a life might look like for you.

Money: The Challenge of Asking Why

The *why* of money is as unique as each individual. Too much of our own interaction with wealth is most often reactive rather than directive. As we've all heard, money makes a wonderful servant but a horrible master.

Yet I firmly believe there are important considerations that warrant thoughtful contemplation and analysis as one's journey with wealth progresses. With this book, I hope to mark a new exploration within the finance and investment literature, something that may best be called wealth strategy. Its key steps are to ground you firmly in understanding wealth in history and how it affects your psychology, help you to define your wealth strategy, and articulate a defined view of how your wealth will be used to build the life you wish to live.

What follows is a guidebook for considerations about what to do with wealth as it comes in and once you've got it. The book can serve as a resource to consult as you deal with the considerations that financial wealth brings into your life. I bring together financial theory, case studies and examples, academic research, and a good dose of common sense. Think of it as the thoughtful contrarian sitting on your own personal board of directors.

This book will ultimately ask a great deal of you, the reader, if you're truly to benefit from the approach it lays out. As we consider wealth in all its facets more deeply, it's important to recognize the need to get outside of oneself and attempt to understand your own thinking. The individual who overworks himself, logging 120 hours a week to accumulate her fortune, labors in service of a goal just as powerful in her life as Bill Gates's choosing to step away from an operational role at Microsoft and give away the vast majority of his fortune in service of the less fortunate.

The key is to understand the implicit and explicit decisions you're making about your life and wealth.

In my undergraduate studies on strategy, one of the key case studies we read was called *What Is Strategy?* by Michael Porter. In it, the famed Harvard Business School professor called attention to the fact that strategy at its core is about choices. Among his insights is the idea that operational excellence is not strategy—meaning that engaging in a particular activity and doing it with excellence, while important, is not a strategic choice.

Strategic articulation is about the conscious choice to engage in some actions and abstain from others. Considerations relating to money function in the same way. We all consciously choose to spend in some ways and not others. But we generally have issues in articulating the choices we're making. Defaults in behavior are incredibly powerful when it comes to finances. Moreover, the clear articulation of the thoughts, values, and emotions that underpin these actions is even more challenging.

In the wealth-management world, the continuing trend in the financial-planning discussion with clients is what's known as *goals-based planning*. It's a shift away from helping the client reach a savings/investment plan by building a household budget and focusing the client's attention instead on what the client would like to see occur. This shift is commendable but highly challenging in reality. Very few families I've worked with can accurately answer where they're spending money today and what they would ideally be spending money on ten, fifteen, or twenty years into the future. Yet to successfully integrate wealth into our lives, we must have a concrete sense of the financial choices we're currently making, know what our priorities are, account for any constraints/considerations, and have a feedback mechanism to measure how we're tracking relative to our strategic plan.

This book is about taking such financial planning and integrating it with life planning. Life planning is about diving deep to understand each of our personal stories and finding out who we are, an exercise that helps us build and create the lives we want. For the wealthy, this dichotomy becomes especially acute because the financial resources available to the individual can very quickly exceed the financial priorities. In the aftermath comes a period of great uncertainty, when new priorities are often built, though they're generally based on peer relationships. What's needed is to reconnect with the life-planning process, so that wealth is integrated into life and drives movement toward a life lived with intention and impact.

I'll walk you through the considerations and process for how you can fully engage with your financial means and use what you learn to construct and live a fulfilling life. These are not easy waters to navigate. Although some considerations are financial or quantitative, many are psychological, sociological, and even spiritual, because they touch on the core elements of what it means to be human.

By the time you've finished the book, you'll have a strategic plan that captures the specific choices/trade-offs about how you'll engage with your wealth and how those choices integrate with and support your values and priorities. You'll also have a mechanism for evaluating the ongoing success or failure of the plan. I believe you'll find the material engaging, with stories, data, charts, and a series of prepared questions designed to spark your thinking. Each chapter is short and digestible in a single sitting, and many end with questions to consider and other suggested resources for learning more. Your task is simply to wade in.

In many ways, fully diving into the subject matter of this book will be a great challenge—not in terms of any technical complexity but simply because of the depth and comprehensiveness of the questions you'll need to answer. But if you're willing to push through to the other side, great joy and rewards await.

CHAPTER 1

WEALTH STRATEGY: DEFINING THE TERMS

"Alice asked the Cheshire Cat who was sitting in a tree,
'What road do I take?'
The cat asked, 'Where do you want to go?'
'I don't know,' answered Alice.
'Then,' said the cat, 'it really doesn't matter, does it?'"

—ALICE'S ADVENTURES IN WONDERLAND

BY LEWIS CARROLL

If we are to undertake the journey of developing and ultimately implementing a wealth strategy, it's essential to consider each of the constituent parts of such a strategy. American economist Michael Porter was really the first to propose a systematic way of evaluating and responding to competition. Perhaps you're familiar with Porter's *five forces* analysis. By carefully analyzing industry structure—including new entrants, suppliers, customers, substitutes, and competitive powers—Porter reasoned that a company could arrive at a strategy for how to win. Similarly, for constructing a wealth strategy, there are two key components to analyze—wealth structure and wealth identity.

Strategy Follows Structure

Strategy is ultimately about selecting from a series of competing choices to articulate a path that's most likely to lead to the accomplishment of a defined goal. To illustrate this, let me step back a few years. During my time at university, I was a business major (focused on entrepreneurship and strategy), minoring in philosophy. Yet almost by happenstance I ended up taking almost as many fine arts classes as philosophy courses.

One of the seminal mental models I learned from my arts courses is how powerfully structure can affect experience. For example, in the fine arts class I took while in London, before we ever visited a gallery, our excellent professor would walk us through an understanding of how the gallery had been organized. Were the works arranged chronologically or by artist? Or perhaps thematically? This seemingly basic concept of the structural arrangement of the works can dramatically affect the way an artist's work is encountered and appreciated.

In the music world, a firm understanding of how the piece is structured can offer the listener greater enjoyment by revealing some order behind the sonic overload. *Strate-*

gy, in its highest form, is not altogether different from a great symphony. Symphonies are beautiful in the aural and melodic elements that pleasantly strike the ear.

Yet there is an even deeper layer of beauty, which can be seen only when the symphony is deconstructed into its component elements. Thus a great symphony can be admired at the level of the individual instrument, and similarly at the level of how each instrument blends with its section and with the orchestra overall.

The key then to strategic analysis is to recognize this tension between the constituent elements and the whole. When building strategy, as when appreciating a symphony, one can consider each of the individual instruments. The instruments join together into orchestral elements, known as sections, that can be arranged to interact with one another. Consider how the woodwinds and the strings may interplay over the course of a piece of music.

Finally, the symphony overall can be considered, such as the time signature of the music. What key is the piece played in? Does the key oscillate or change? How is harmony used? What about dissonance? Each of those elements interplays to deliver the experience.

The symphony analogy can be helpful as we consider what strategy looks like in relation to wealth. Much like the elements involved in an orchestral piece, four significant structural elements must come together as we construct a wealth strategy:

1. conditions and resources

2. level of wealth
3. psychology
4. how we make or lose financial wealth

What follows is a quick summary of each element, but we'll look in greater depth at each one in the coming chapters and walk you through the analysis needed to create the raw material for creating a wealth strategy.

1. Conditions and Resources

The starting place of any strategy is to consider the big external factors that may be influencing the situation. In the business world, these conditions are known as PEST—the political, environmental, social, and technological elements that can affect the business. These elements are just as relevant for individuals and families. In our current environment, with wealth inequality at peak levels, the broader attitude of the wealthy toward the middle and lower classes is under great scrutiny, arguably as much as it was with the Robber Barons of the early 1900s.

With an understanding of external conditions, the natural next step is to look at wealth in its most functional orientation—in actual dollars and cents. Yet, is wealth ultimately related only to financial assets? Or does it encapsulate something more than that?

To answer this, it's best to reference Jay Hughes's work described in *Family Wealth: Keeping It In the Family*. The book was written to help families explore the roots for the curse of shirtsleeves to shirtsleeves in three generations, the global proverb that highlights the transient nature of wealth. In understanding the root causes of the malady and a potential prescription for avoiding its ill effects, Hughes makes the case that when families reduce their wealth to only its financial element, they sow the seeds for the ultimate demise of the family fortune.

Hughes encourages families to consider instead a more holistic concept of wealth, one that encapsulates its many forms, of which financial wealth is only one component. The other forms of wealth (or *capital*, to use Hughes's term), which we all possess, include human, intellectual, spiritual, and social capital.

Intellectual capital is the knowledge and learning we gain through our education and life experience. Spiritual capital represents the values and heritage that come from our own faith practice and possibly the faith heritage of our family. Social capital captures how one relates to the broader society as a whole. Finally, human capital considers the values, dreams, and aspirations of the family.

By expanding the definition of wealth beyond just the financial, Hughes encourages us to recognize the breadth of resources we bring to bear as we navigate through life's challenges. Financial capital is a necessary but insufficient component to living life well; in and of itself, it is inadequate in solving all of life's concerns.

2. Level of Wealth

Building upon the conditions and resources a family has, the next helpful step is to calibrate those resources. We next consider the level of the family's wealth and some high-level considerations that come into play as the wealth grows over time. The purpose of this analysis is to set expectations based on the big questions that come into play and to normalize the uniqueness of the experience of having higher levels of wealth.

3. Psychology

As the individual or family reckons with its wealth, we're working with the notion that *we have met the enemy, and the enemy is us.* For much of modern history, economists have assumed that the "economic man" was rational in his behavior. Only recently has the field of behavioral economics begun to articulate a competing view, understanding how the brain actually behaves when making financial decisions.

To articulate a wealth strategy that has a chance at winning, we will have to face our own psychology—head on. Chapter 4, "Psychology, Money's War on Our Brains," covers this in much greater detail.

4. How We Make or Lose Financial Wealth

The final element considers the path by which we came into wealth. There are numerous pathways to wealth—from the lucky lottery winner, to the unlucky victim (say the target of a product liability lawsuit), to the entrepreneur or inheritor. Each of these paths brings a series of opportunities and threats that we must consider before we can deploy the wealth well.

Strategy Is Powered by Identity

We've outlined the major components of wealth structure. These structural elements for both the foundation and guardrails shape the strategy in much the same way that the foundation, walls, and girders form the outline of what a building could look like. Yet, the building's ultimate shape is informed and powered by something else—the architect's ability to take the parts and create something beautiful.

The next section of the book wrestles with what we call *wealth identity*. Identity and self are complicated topics and it's not my intention to get weighed down in a hundred years of psychological research and debate. Instead, I outline the major constituent elements as levers for your thinking, but I ultimately encourage the engagement of a professional coach (if you're feeling stuck) or counselor (if you're wrestling with real trauma).

Knowing oneself is only the first half of what's involved in wealth identity. The second half is just as important and represents the first step in constructing a wealth strategy. This second half is about making a first set of positive affirmations about your core purpose (or *why*), core values (how you will conduct yourself), and finally a vision of what the future could look like if your *why* and *value* are being lived out.

Conclusion

Only with a strong understanding your wealth's structure and a keen sense of your wealth identity are you ready to begin making the really strategic choices of a wealth strategy. The strategy itself looks at blending those key inputs into a set of guiding principles around consumption, investment, philanthropy, and giving to future generations—the four primary choices the wealthy must make about where their assets will be directed.

SECTION ONE

WEALTH STRUCTURE

CHAPTER 2

WEALTH AND WHAT IT IS

*"Money brings some happiness. But after a
certain point, it just brings more money."*

—NEIL SIMON

---

et's look now in greater detail at what wealth is and
what it means to carry the label *wealthy*. At this point,
we will consider only financial resources in the definition of wealth. That is not to dismiss other forms of wealth,
which you will see later on I consider extremely important, but rather to explore the most common definitions of
wealth.

I present the question *Am I rich?* because it captures
several of the common responses to the question of wealth.
First, some are confused about whether or not they qualify
as wealthy. Second, many are on the outside looking in,
either desiring their own wealth but unsure how to get it
or expecting its eventual presence in their life. The third

reaction is a common one, of almost disbelief at the state of one's finances. Whether due to an unanticipated inheritance, an investment that pans out better than expected, or even just smart, thrifty living and savings over time, it's common in my experience to interact with folks who find themselves in much different financial circumstances than they had ever planned on achieving.

Am I Rich? Who Qualifies as Wealthy?

To remove potential ambiguity, let's define what *wealthy* means here in the United States. There are a couple of different ways we can consider it. First, consider how those who work with the wealthy answer the question. After all, the chance to make a dollar has a profound ability to sharpen the mind about such matters. The broader financial services industry typically categorizes clients into four main buckets based on the size of their pool investable assets:

- ➤ mass market, with net worth less than $100 thousand
- ➤ mass affluent, with net worth between $100 thousand and $1 million
- ➤ high net worth, ranging from $1 million to $20 million
- ➤ ultra high net worth, with more than $20 million

In my professional experience, the high-net-worth and ultra-high-net-worth categories define those we consider wealthy.

Second, academic research can be helpful in answering the question. In 2016, Emmanuel Saez and Gabriel Zucman, professors of economics at the University of California, Berkeley, published a phenomenal paper entitled "Wealth Inequality in the United States Since 1913: Evidence From Capitalized Income Tax Data" in *The Quarterly Journal of Economics*. What was unique about Saez and Zucman's paper was how they used income tax returns to examine various taxes paid and then estimated the balance sheet of various households. For example, they note that 90 percent of American households have an average net worth of $84,000. The top 1 to 0.1 percent, or 1.45 million households in the U.S., have an average net worth of $7.3 million, with a minimum net worth of $3.9 million.

TABLE 1

Thresholds and Average Wealth in Top Wealth Groups, 2012

Wealth group	No. of Families	Wealth threshold	Average wealth	Wealth Share
PANEL A: TOP WEALTH GROUPS				
Full Population	160,700,00		$343,000	100%
Top 10%	16,070,00	$660,000	$2,560,000	77.2%
Top 1%	1,607,00	$3,960,000	$13,840,000	41.8%
Top .1%	160,700	$20,600,000	$72,800,000	22.0%
Top .01%	16,070	$111,000,000	$371,000,000	11.2%
PANEL B: INTERMEDIATE WEALTH GROUPS				
Bottom 90%	144,600,000		$84,000	22.8%
Top 10-1%	14,463,000	$660,000	$1,310,000	35.4%
Top 1-0.1%	1,446,300	$3,960,000	$7,290,000	19.8%
Top 0.1-0.01%	144,600	$20,6000,000	$39,700,000	10.8%
Top .01%	16,070	$111,000,000	$371,000,000	11.2%

Notes. This table reports statistics on the wealth distribution in the United States in 2012 obtained by capitalizing income tax returns. The unit in the family (either a single person aged 20 or above or a married couple, in both cases with children dependents if any). Fractiles are defined relatively to the total number of families in the population. Source: Online Appendix Table B1.

EXHIBIT 2.1

So, for our purposes, it is reasonable to consider someone as reasonably wealthy once they climb into the top 10
percent (that is, at least $660 thousand in assets). At that
level, saving and investing practices outstrip consumption,
which allows for the continued increase in assets as time
passes. As you can see in Exhibit 2.2, as net worth increases, a person's savings rate actually increases as a percentage
of their income.

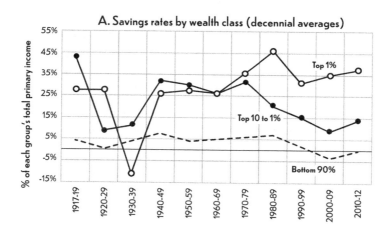

EXHIBIT 2.2

While the data would be supportive that being in the top
10 percent would make someone wealthy, in reality that is
not likely to be the level in America where one feels particularly wealthy. For the purposes of this book, we will focus
on the top 1 percent of wealth holders, with a minimum
threshold of $3.9 million—especially the top 0.1 percent,
with a minimum of $20.6 million.

Income Does Not Equal Wealth; Nor Is It the Source of Most Wealth

Having a high income does not in fact make you wealthy. Income is the annual stream of cash flow received from your professional activities. It may be helpful to visualize income as a flowing river of water. Wealth is an accumulated pool of income, accomplished by diverting some of this annual stream until it becomes a lake.

Determining how much income to direct toward funding wealth is a balancing act between choosing to consume now or accumulate assets that allow consumption at a later date—either in your lifetime during retirement or much further on, if assets are passed to the next generation for their benefit.

Income does not equal wealth and, accordingly, high income does not mean significant wealth. While that sounds obvious, it's all too common for a lawyer with a super high income or a doctor who may be pulling in a high-six-figure or low-seven-figure annual salary to consider themselves wealthy. To which, the best answer is *wait and see.* Such professionals have high human capital—that is, the potential earnings someone generates over the course of a working career. We'll explore human capital in greater detail later on, but think of it for now as an asset that exists off the balance sheet, which has been generated as a result of formal education and the development of a unique, valuable skill set that's well compensated by the marketplace.

Human capital is a store of potential value that converts into bank account dollars with each pay period that passes. All too often, folks with high human capital believe themselves wealthy and act as if they are. They can fund a lifestyle similar to that of the wealthy because they generate the cash flow necessary to support the expenditures. The reasoning follows along these lines: *I am a brain surgeon who makes $850,000 annually; there is no reason I shouldn't have a 6,000-square-foot home, two Mercedes in the driveway, and a beach home.* Never mind the fact that almost universally there are large student loans to pay and low retirement-account balances relative to age/stage of life.

Although they're able to meet the cash flow requirements of owning such assets, can we consider large debt balances of mortgage and car notes to be ownership? I think not. In reality, such individuals are debt financing a lifestyle rather than accumulating an asset base that ultimately can begin to self-fund such consumption. The key difference is that true wealth occurs when the wealth can compound independently of effort.

Wealth for the vast majority of the top 1 percent of net worth is generated through the steady diversion of income into investment accounts. With the continued incremental contributions that come from steady savings—and assistance from the wondrous power of compound interest— wealth can accumulate to fund one's lifestyle, in many cases in perpetuity without having to spend down principal balances. For a meaningful portion of the populace, this is how they will come into wealth.

Those few that enter the top 0.1 percent of wealth generate their fortune in different ways. We will talk about common paths to the *ultra high net-worth* status in Chapter 7, "Defining Your Wealth Identity."

Oh, No, I'm Rich

I hope, with some of this additional data, you have been able to identify your level of wealth. There is often a cognitive disconnect between how one feels about their wealth versus what the absolute level of wealth would indicate. For example, someone with a net worth of $50 million in East Hampton may not feel particularly wealthy, given the peer group surrounding them. And attaining the status of wealthy brings with it a whole additional set of considerations, many of which may never have been considered before:

- What is wealth really?
- Why did we want wealth in the first place? And does wealth actually satisfy that underlying desire?
- Can we lose it? What does security mean to us? How does money fit into that plan, or does it? (Survey data indicates that millionaires report needing twice their level of wealth to feel secure.)
- What is required to manage this newfound pool of resources?

→ Are there expectations for my behavior that accompany this wealth? For example, if it's received
as an inheritance?

→ How much of this wealth belongs to me? What
responsibility do I feel toward my current family,
future generations, the broader community, and
the world?

For most who ultimately come to possess significant levels
of financial capital, there generally was a time when they
did not possess financial wealth. The reasons we desired
wealth in the first place will likely inform the direction we
take in defining its roles and uses now that we have it.

It's important to consider as well how that underlying
motivation may adapt or be forced to change. Consider
the person who labored tirelessly to acquire wealth as a way
of avoiding being destitute, or to avoid the fate of a family
member who lost a significant fortune due to bad luck or
mismanagement. The obvious example here is the character
Mr. Crawley in *Downton Abbey*, who manages to lose the
entire Crawley family fortune through poor investments.

For the person whose efforts were driven by the fear
of going broke, suddenly having plenty can easily be disorienting. At a certain level of assets, the balances in an
investment account could be invested in relatively low-
risk options such as Treasury bills or high-quality munic-
ipal bonds, with the income from such investments more
than covering cash flow needs. The risk from this portfolio

would arguably be so low that it's hard to foresee a way in which the wealth would be lost irrevocably.

For example, I met several years ago with the shrewd CEO who had managed to successfully steer his company through two rounds of private equity ownership, ultimately to sell the company to a large publicly traded competitor. This individual had made more money than he'd ever imagined. Taking the cash proceeds and investing them in a low-return portfolio of highly conservative bonds would have produced income far beyond the standard of living the CEO was comfortable with at the time. Although he relished the new role of being able to hire/fire an advisor, and likely enjoyed the attention of having many firms calling to seek his business, he ultimately was at his wits' end about what to do next. Much like the dog chasing the bus, very little thought had been given to what happens after wealth is attained.

What Is My Role in Managing Wealth? What Are My Responsibilities?

As the saying goes, *To whom much is given, much is required.* Managing a sizable investment pool brings with it a series of new considerations: vetting and selecting an investment advisor, addressing new tax considerations, choosing a competent trust and estates counsel.

To some, such nitty-gritty details are fascinating and of great interest. But in my experience, for most, it's an unwelcome experience, like that of the widow—after the passing of a beloved husband—who's suddenly forced to consider the financial matters of the family for the first time. Or like the middle-aged daughter who unexpectedly inherits $20 million in a trust after the passing of her father.

An interesting fact to note about wealth is that having it is not a permanent state of affairs. Wealth counselor and advisor James Grubman highlights a number of key points about the wealthy in his book *Strangers in Paradise*. First, he points out that 80 percent of the wealthy become so during their lifetime—that is, they're not born to wealth. As such, the ranks of the wealthy are in constant flux. Although some families are able to avoid the proverb of *shirtsleeves to shirtsleeves in three generations,* those who constitute society's wealthy are not a static group but rather in constant flux. So it's reasonable to surmise, as Grubman does, that the state of being wealthy is for many a temporary one, with numbers of people reaching its status for the first time just as many others lose that status.

Despite this pace of change, there are very few resources available to assist folks in navigating their way through the land of the wealthy. Grubman, both in his book and in his work with wealthy clients, views coming to wealth as analogous to a family that lives a native land and immigrates to a new one. When they leave their culture of origin, they arrive in a new world where some things are similar, but many are new. Their task is to acculturate to their new surroundings and begin the hard work of preparing future generations to remain in the new land, if the family is to stay in its new home.

This is a largely unclear process—hence why I wrote this book. As Grubman notes, "The greatest mistake many newcomers [to wealth] make is that they believe they already know the roadmap for adapting to wealth, but they would be wrong."

CHAPTER 3

LEVEL OF WEALTH

"The other day we saw a mouse in the house. Before, I would have just gotten a broom and gotten rid of the thing. But now it's different. I emailed the household manager. He called the vendor, a pest-control firm, and the pest-control firm caught the mouse. Then the household manager directed two other staff members to dispose of the mouse. That's five people to catch a mouse. It all seemed normal at the time. But then I thought about it, and I wondered, how did our lives get like this?"

—ROBERT FRANK, *RICHISTAN*

S everal years ago, I was at a conference for family offices. At a happy hour one night, I struck up a conversation with the head of a family office for a billionaire family. This individual remarked that even if given the chance, he would never want to trade places with his client. Here he was, supporting someone with a ten-figure net worth, and most likely well compensated himself. But having looked at life on the other side of the desk, this advisor did not feel the trade-off was worth it. He believed the complexity and stress that come from being exceptionally wealthy are not accompanied by benefits proportionally as great.

As we consider how best to live with our wealth, it's important to consider this dynamic of marginal benefit as the absolute level of wealth increases. This ties in closely with psychology. How we think about the significance of various levels of wealth is heavily influenced by the factors at play at each level.

As we discussed in Chapter 2, "Wealth and What It Means," there are four general levels of net worth toward which the financial services industry generally directs its marketing. Here we'll consider a few characteristics for each level and consider one special case.

Less Than $100,000 of Investable Assets

Known as the mass market, the vast majority of American households fall into this category. Some may be in this category because they've only just begun accumulating wealth. Many others are in this category because of high levels of debt, poor spending habits, and/or bad luck perhaps due to health emergencies. At this stage, engaging thoughtfully with wealth is tied largely to prudent cash flow management and gearing spending levels appropriately.

Please note that if you're in this stage, you should understand that the mass market is not the subject of this book. Feel free to read on to understand the sorts of questions and considerations that may await you as you climb the wealth ladder. For more relevant advice to your particular circumstances, we commend traditional materials like Dave Ramsey's *Financial Peace* as a helpful set of tools and strategies for managing wealth at this stage.

More Than $100,000 but Less Than $1 Million

At this stage, the household is considered among the mass affluent. Although they are climbing the path toward wealth through savings accumulation and some investments, the overall considerations at this stage are more or less relatively straightforward.

These folks focus on managing consumption to allow regular ongoing investments to the financial markets. The time value of money and the power of compound interest are their friends. To the extent they have time, this program of reasonable living and ongoing contributions will see their accounts grow steadily over time. Beyond that, it's worthwhile keeping in mind the right structure of investments to make sure that the portfolio is not taking on unnecessary levels of risk. One common framework for evaluating this is to look at three buckets of assets. The first bucket, *safety assets* such as cash or very short-term bonds, which could cover spending in market volatility. The second, *market assets,* are broadly diversified across geography and asset class to capture market returns at the lowest possible cost. Market assets are designed to enable spending to keep up with inflation over time. The final *bucket* is aspirational assets—which carry higher risk and higher potential returns that could have a transformative effect on personal spending if they pan out. For the mass affluent, making sure enough risk is being taken—but not too much—is a paramount concern.

One thing we see regularly among mass affluent individuals and families is that they simply do not save enough to be able to reach their goals. J.P. Morgan Asset Management produces a helpful guide to retirement each year, which walks through a number of considerations for long-term planning. A favorite chart (see Exhibit 3.1) looks at the level of savings that someone should have accumulated for various levels of household income in order to be on track to retire and be able to replace the necessary level of income for maintaining a similar standard of living.

Current Age	$30,000	$40,000	$50,000	$60,000	$70,000	$80,000	$90,000
			Checkpoint (x current household income)				
25	0.4	0.4	0.5	0.6	0.8	0.9	1.1
30	0.7	0.8	0.9	1.0	1.2	1.4	1.5
35	1.1	1.2	1.3	1.5	1.7	2.0	2.1
40	1.6	1.8	1.9	2.0	2.4	2.6	2.9
45	2.2	2.4	2.5	2.7	3.1	3.5	3.7
50	3.0	3.2	3.3	3.6	4.1	4.5	4.8
55	3.9	4.1	4.3	4.6	5.2	5.7	6.1
60	4.9	5.2	5.5	5.8	6.6	7.2	7.6
65	6.4	6.8	7.0	7.5	8.4	9.1	9.7

How to use:
- This analysis assumes you would like to maintain an equivalent lifestyle in retirement.
- Household income is assumed to be gross income (before taxes and savings).
- Go to the intersection of your current age and your closest current household income.
- Multiply your salary by the checkpoint shown. This is the amount you should have saved today, assuming you continue contributions of 5% going forward.
- Example: For a 40-year-old with a household income of $50,000: $50,000 x 1.9 = $95,000

EXHIBIT 3.1

This analysis assumes that the individual saves only 5 percent of income going forward. In my own experience building long-range financial plans for families, they may not have accumulated anywhere near these levels yet, so instead of 5 percent savings going forward, they likely need to be at the 15-20 percent range in order to catch up to where they need to be. Although a 15 percent savings rate sounds difficult, with most employers domestically matching retirement contributions anywhere from 3-6 percent, a 15 percent savings goal is functionally more like a 10 percent target.

One way to consider reaching this goal would be to start at the level of maximum match, that is, if the company will match 50 percent up to 6 percent of the employee's pay, begin by saving 6 percent to capture the maximum match (this is free money!). This translates to a 9 percent savings rate. Then, going forward, commit to directing a fixed amount of every increase in salary toward growing this savings rate.

So hypothetically, you would commit ex-ante (and some plans now allow this as an option) to give 1 percent of every raise toward savings. So if you get a 3 percent cost-of-living increase, you would increase take-home pay by 2 percent and set aside 1 percent toward retirement. By building this way, the savings rate is reached in short order, but its effect on cash flow is muted. Of course, big promotions and other potential step changes in earnings power are great places to get to the right savings rate. There is still a nice boost in income, but also a chance to hit an appropriate savings goal.

$1 Million to $20 Million

Households with $1 million to $20 million are in the traditional high-net-worth segment. Households in this bracket are in a somewhat interesting place. At a high level, the overall complexity of the households is reasonably manageable. Although there may be several investment accounts, likely a taxable Roth IRA and various deferred vehicles such as 401(k) plans and rollover IRAs from prior employees, there are most likely few other structures utilized.

With current estate planning laws allowing $11 million in lifetime exemption for individuals and $22 million for couples, it's good to be proactive in planning going forward, but there are not likely to be any major substantive estate-planning issues to address that would dramatically increase the complexity of the household. All this is good news for the high-net-worth household.

The bad news is that these households probably do require the most planning to avoid taking excess risks and to avoid outliving their assets. These households are most exposed to the risk of being forced to take meaningful withdrawals from retirement accounts during periods of market stress, which have an outsized effect because these withdrawals eat into the principal balance of the account. These withdrawals limit the amount of capital available to grow over time. The family's human capital/earnings power also becomes depleted as middle and old age begin, which limits the replenishment potential. Carefully planning spending and looking at the flexibility of one's expenditures are helpful in managing the longer-term risk.

$20 Million to $100 Million+— the Ultra High Net Worth

The difference between the top 1 percent and top 0.1 percent is sizable. As noted in Chapter 2, on wealth, the top 1 percent have an average net worth of around $13 million, obviously skewed by the higher end. One enters the 0.1

percent with a net worth of $20.6 million, with an average net worth of $72.8 million.

In my experience the key word in working with families in this range is *complexity*. Although the top 1 percent likely have a very high standard of living and arguably want for very little, the change as the net worth levels climb is that for the most part any remaining restrictions on consumption go by the wayside.

Of course, there is always someone else with more, and even for the highest end, there are always the sheiks and Russian billionaires near the top. But at $40 to $50 million, it's not unreasonable for the common signifiers of the ultra high net worth to begin appearing—private jets, multiple residences, yachts, and the like. Although toys such as these may serve a life-enhancing function, they also represent a meaningful increase in complexity. In owning such assets, individuals may be dealing with multi-state and country issues surrounding residency, titling, and household help. Accompanying such a rise in wealth is likely an increase in prominence socially, whether desired or not. This may bring along a whole host of unplanned for security and privacy concerns.

Families of such means may begin establishing family foundations or making sizable commitments. As we'll discuss at much greater length in Chapter 12, "Philanthropy," giving at this level and wanting to see levels of philanthropic efficacy similar to those they're accustomed to in their business holdings may lead them to develop a comprehensive framework for evaluating social sector change.

Moreover, for many in these circumstances, the money simply cannot be spent in a single lifetime. Families may shift their goals to benefiting future generations. Of course, there is a tax imperative to minimize the potential for estate taxes. Yet overarching even that is likely a desire to see such financial resources used for good and not ill in future generations.

We have mentioned the proverb of *shirtsleeves to shirtsleeves in three generations*. Arguably, no person who has built a sizable fortune wants such a prophecy to befall his family. Building the right legal structures and arming them with the right trustees, who can serve as mentors and guides to those who benefit from the largesse of prior generations, are critical tasks.

Investment advice in this sector becomes a bit of a challenge. The choice simply becomes whether to be a big fish in a smaller pond or a small fish in a big pond. Although such levels of wealth, complexity, and sophistication will easily outstrip the background and capability of many a local firm, the question of where to place one's business looms larger. The private banking divisions of larger financial institutions such as Goldman Sachs and J.P. Morgan are natural partners. Specialty trust companies like Bessemer Trust or Northern Trust are possibilities as well. Finally, there are a number of specialty asset managers, like

Hirtle Callahan, Greystone, and Glenmede, who focus on many of these families.

Other families may choose to partner with a multi-family office (MFO), an en vogue concept wherein the traditional service suite of a single-family office (SFO) is opened more broadly to a select group of families. At the risk of standing on a soapbox, allow me to quickly dispel one myth. Because a firm pays your bills and may book a dinner reservation, that does not make it a family office. Those are nice services to have and likely can make life easier, but a family office is just that—focused on the needs of the family. The signifiers in my mind of the true family office are as follows:

- ➼ **Selective focus.** These firms may only seek to add one or two client relationships a year. Family offices looking to grow aggressively may be good at sales/ business development, but they're making compromises elsewhere.

- ➼ **High-touch service**. Keep in mind their predecessor firms, the single-family office. Because SFOs serve a single constituency, they're run to a net-zero profit target. They can offer the services they offer because they're run at cost. A true multi-family office should be a great business for the clients, not the owners of the MFO.

- ➼ **Integration.** The family's tax, legal, investment, and other matters should be coordinated under one roof. Although I don't believe the MFO has to draft trust documents in house to be accurately called an MFO, it must be the one taking the lead. Here is another telltale sign of the MFO. When taxes are due, or financial or life circumstances change, who takes the lead in initiating a conversation? The family or the firm? If the firm is leading, that's a family office.

→ **Discretion.** Most family offices are focused on quiet service for their client. They are created because the family wants to narrow the circle of folks who are in the know about the family's business. If other clients of a firm talk about their family office on the tee box, chances are it's not a family office. This high need for status signaling becomes the primary service delivered for many clients of the flash nouveau family office.

More Than $100 Million

The final segmentation of the levels of wealth is the top 0.1 percent—the tip of the wealth pyramid. If the key word for the last segment was *complexity*, I would argue that the key word here is *scale*. Although the numbers are certainly bigger in this range, with average net worth of $375 million, the difference between someone with $50 million and $350 million is that the person with $350 million can, in effect, build a business to focus on the needs of the one person/family. With a 1 percent fee budget, an operating

budget of $3.5 million annually can pay for a chief invest-
ment officer, tax accountant, etc., focused entirely on the
needs of one family. At $50 million—although $500,000
of fee budget is nothing to sneeze at—market rate talent
for a chief investment officer is likely around $750,000 to
$1,000,000. Therefore, the top 0.1 percent can largely turn
the oversight and management of their lives and financial
resources over to an institution capable of hiring the caliber
of talent required to effectively manage those sums well.
Of course, all the complexity of the prior level remains and
continues to increase. The choice to build a family office
is also a choice to begin building a second business that's
very different in nature from the business that generated
the family's wealth.

CHAPTER 4

PSYCHOLOGY: MONEY'S WAR ON OUR BRAINS

"A foolish consistency is the hobgoblin of little minds."

—RALPH WALDO EMERSON

A key assumption underlying the entirety of this book is that much of how we think about—and, as a result, use—our money is suboptimal in some capacity. Human beings are fickle creatures and can be blown by the wind, as is well demonstrated by the whims of fashion trends that come and go. And yet, interestingly, for most of the history of economics as a social science with dedicated academic practitioners, man was presumed to be a rational actor when faced with making decisions about money.

The work of the last twenty to thirty years in a field known as behavioral finance has shown in great light the limits of human rationality. This work has been so transformative that it has resulted in Daniel Kahneman's, the Israeli-American economist and psychologist, and arguably the godfather of the discipline, receiving the Nobel Prize in Economics Sciences. Kahneman has written about his research in great length and published the best-selling *Thinking Fast and Slow,* in which he does a tremendous job of walking the layperson through his major findings. Journalist Michael Lewis, in his book *The Undoing Project,* tells the story of Kahneman and his research colleague Amos Tversky.

Given the number of books available on the subject, it seems foolish to try to cover at length here the tremendous work that has been done in the field. At the end of the chapter, you'll find a list of relevant books offering more information. Instead, I want to distill seven key principles that are worth keeping in mind as we consider decision-making around our wealth.

PRINCIPLE 1

How We Made It Matters

We've all heard the Proverb 13:11—"Wealth gained hastily [or by fraud] will dwindle, but whoever gathers little by little will increase it." Written somewhere close to 2,500 years ago, the Hebrew book of wisdom literature known as *Proverbs* is quick to point out two different ways by which wealth is accumulated. The Teacher, as the author refers to himself, contrasts hastily gained money and money "gathered little by little." This truth is as relevant today as it was back then, except today the stakes seem only higher. When Powerball and Mega Millions jackpot totals regularly approach and exceed the $500 million mark, for the lucky few, great wealth can be gained hastily in today's world.

One does not have to play the lottery to face the challenge of hasty wealth. The most recent crop of crypto-currency millionaires (and potentially billionaires) are likely in the same boat. The problems with gaining money quickly are many.

First, we don't think clearly about the receipt of money we didn't expect to have. Economists refer to the permanent income hypothesis when they discuss how tax cuts might affect consumer spending. This hypothesis states that people spend money based on their long-term assessment of their income potential. That's why short-term stimulative measures for an economy are generally not successful in affecting consumer spending over the long-term. So if our default manner of assessing our spending is based on our long-term income potential, when we have a major event that results in unexpected income, we think about our wealth using a different rubric known as *found money*.

Found money is a beautiful thing; we all love it when it occurs. It's the proverbial twenty-dollar bill we find hiding in a pair of jeans we haven't worn in a while or tucked into a seat cushion. When we receive found money, the research is quite conclusive that we spend it very quickly. The reason for this is that we've already seen to our regular needs (and some wants) in the course of our budgeting/mental accounting from our regular income sources. When found money arrives, it's unexpected and outside of this prior assessment. As such, we can spend it guilt-free because we were not planning on having it anyway.

So imagine a schoolteacher, making $50,000 a year, who suddenly wins $100 million from the Powerball jackpot. She simply has no rubric to evaluate such a sum because it far eclipses the prior levels of expected spending. As such, it's easy to fall into a shopping-spree mindset. That, combined with the inevitable hangers-on who come out of the woodwork to gain from the fortune, it's not surprising how quickly large sums can disappear. It's not just lottery winners who are at risk here. Professional sports is littered with stories with the same outcome.

PRINCIPLE 2

The Amount Matters Too

The level of wealth received makes a difference too. If someone is used to a $500,000 a year lifestyle, has $8 million in investments, and suddenly receives an additional $5 million, you may see some change in behavior, but likely not much. Although $5 million to some folks represents a staggering amount, to someone who already has a high net worth, that additional $5 million is nice to have but likely not a transformative amount because it's unlikely to enable them to lift their standard of living to whatever they feel is the next level up the ladder.

This means that how we think about wealth is always affected by what we think about the amount and, more important, what we think about the amount relative to our current spending levels or, I would add, our own past conception.

As a result, in my experience, it's common to begin thinking about wealth in break-point levels. Here are a few examples to consider. A mid-thirties vice president works at a decent-sized public company, has a total net worth of about $1 million, and makes $250,000 in cash compensation annually. This VP has organized a standard of living in relation to her current level of spending and also considering the path of future promotions. She looks down her own career path and considers a move toward becoming a senior or executive vice president, with a total compensation package approaching $1 million annually.

Now take a step back and consider whether $1 million annually is a large or small amount. Here is where background matters. If our vice president is from a small town and is, say, the child of a local schoolteacher who married a policeman—both solid, middle-class professions—$1 million a year may appear to be a having *made it*.

Now let's consider an inverted scenario. The CEO of a public company has a $2 million annual cash compensation arrangement and has $15 million in his 401(k) and equity ownership in the company. This CEO arranges a sale of the business and pockets, say, $20 million all in after a change in control provisions in her employment contract, bringing the total liquid net worth to $35-$40 million. After buying the lawyer who negotiated the contract a bottle of Johnnie Walker Blue, the now former CEO ponders life ahead. Nearing sixty, he decides to become an operating partner for a local private equity firm, lending his considerable background, operating acumen, and robust Rolodex to the firm's efforts. In exchange for that, and perhaps a more modest twenty-hour-a-week commitment, the fund pays the CEO $1 million a year.

Arguably in this hypothetical scenario, this individual is going to view the same dollar amount very differently. First, the pay level will feel like a cut because it's below his prior level of income. Moreover, depending how lifestyle spending has been arranged, the $1 million a year may require him to make some distributions from his investment portfolio to support annual spending.

Although these two cases may seem self-evident, I believe they demonstrate an important point for Principle 2—that amounts of money and how we view them are affected by a number of different factors:

+ upbringing
+ geography of residence—in many locales, there is frankly only a finite amount of money that can be spent, even after buying the large house, nice country club membership, etc.

➤ stage in life when the cash flow occurs
➤ sequence of how the money is accumulated relative to the overall path of earnings.

PRINCIPLE 3

Losing Always Feels Worse

This principle seems so obvious that you may read it and wonder *so what?* Yet what may seem common sense to you and me has proved to be revolutionary in the world of behavioral finance. At the risk of bringing up bad memories, recall your Economics 101 class in college, which assumed that individuals calmly and coolly assessed their various alternatives when making choices and then engaged in a decision-making process known as utility maximization. The idea held that we ultimately will make a selection based on whatever option provides the most bang for the buck. This is also known as risk aversion. To be risk averse means that we attempt to think through the risks of a decision and then decide that the gain must adequately compensate for the risk incurred to get there, or, perhaps better stated, the juice must be worth the squeeze.

Behavioral finance turns this on its head and says that, in fact, we are not risk averse but rather are loss averse. We will go to exceptional lengths to avoid experiencing financial losses. This manifests itself in a number of different ways. For some, this may mean continuing to double down when at the casino, in hopes that one roll of the dice will allow us to win back what we've lost. We see this regularly in the financial markets as people hesitate to sell their losers and hold on to their winners for far too long.

One realization I quickly came to when running a hedge fund is that the winners never felt proportionally as good as how bad our losers felt. When picking stocks, you really only need to be right a little more than 50 percent of the time. If you can manage your downside risk well, so that your losers don't overly cost the portfolio, it's possible to build a tremendous track record with a hit ratio in that range.

Although I knew this to be true, ultimately it was never that simple. A stock that went down 20 percent shortly after buying into it is a perplexing thing. If you're a value investor, you always assume that you're not going to buy the stock at its lowest trade point. But choosing to realize a loss and limit the negative impact to the portfolio is undermined by fear of missing out and what may happen before you're able to buy back in again. Moreover, choosing when to buy back in is never an easy task. This behavior reinforces the idea that when we're faced with realizing losses, our financial decision-making remains consistently suboptimal.

PRINCIPLE 4

Beware the Drug Addict's Curse— Hedonic Adaptation

We're all familiar with the concept that drug addicts require ever higher levels of their drug of choice to experience the same high they had previously. This phenomenon, known as hedonic adaptation, affects well-functioning adults as well.

I have two favorite examples of how this plays out. First was a demonstration I was once asked to perform in a class. The teacher asked us to roll down our sleeves and pull out a clean piece of paper. Next we were to take a pencil and sketch out the face of our watches from memory. Finally, we were asked to compare our actual watch face to the picture drawn. What was so surprising to me and many others was how widely the memory diverged from reality. Here was a physical object we wore on our wrists and might look at upwards of twenty times a day, and yet it was hard to recall what it looked like in firm detail.

Consider as well what occurs after you purchase a new piece of art for a wall of your home. For the first few days after its arrival, each time you walk past the piece or even the room it's in, you stop to admire your new purchase. Yet, over time, the painting will somehow fade into the background, becoming part of the backdrop of everyday life.

All this demonstrates that even with positive stimuli, we grow accustomed to the old and yearn for the new.

The reward centers of our brain lose their sensitivity to the dopamine rush of the novel. As Wang, Novemsky, and Dhar note in their 2009 paper "Anticipating Adaption to Products," "Consumers often fail to predict diminishing product enjoyment over time. Moreover, we show that this failure to predict hedonic adaptation to products arises not because of erroneous beliefs about how experienced utility changes over time but rather because of a failure to incorporate largely correct beliefs about adaptation at the moment of choice."

Not only do we adapt; we fail to consider such adaption into our decision-making and can become even more dissatisfied with our purchases when this natural cycle occurs. This principle of hedonic adaptation undergirds a warning that a life whose enjoyment and happiness are defined by novelty and consumption will likely spin more and more out of control, due to the near-constant need to accumulate more.

PRINCIPLE 5

Robbing Peter to Pay Paul—the Challenge of Delayed Gratification

Not only do we experience hedonic adaptation, we regularly rob Peter to pay Paul and avoid delaying gratification to an alarming degree. As is regularly commented in the press, large portions of the U.S. population have less than

$500 immediately available in the event of an emergency. This is echoed by similar statistics regarding overall levels of retirement savings. The most important takeaway here is that we struggle to balance competing priorities, that is, the important and urgent and the important but not urgent.

Atul Gawande, in his book *Being Mortal*, highlights that the reason for this is found in the work of Stanford psychologist Laura Carstensen. Carstensen's key hypothesis—also known as "socioemotional selectivity theory"—is that "how we seek to spend our time may depend on how much time we perceive ourselves to have." When our time horizon (that is, proximity to death) shortens, the choices we make and things we prioritize change dramatically. Conversely, when our time horizon extends, those choices return to prior priorities.

Because life is perceived to be long and retirement many years in the distance, we naturally do not want to prioritize delaying gratification in order to provide for future needs.

PRINCIPLE 6

Mental Accounting—You May Not Have a Budget but You Do Keep Mental Accounts (Also, We All Have Slippery Categories)

Mental accounting is a fascinating phenomenon we all engage in. The quick synopsis is that we all mentally segment our money into various accounts. We know that X amount of the monthly income goes to cover the mortgage and Y amount will go to cover food. Even if we don't explicitly engage in monthly budgeting, we all generally have a sense of how much money is coming in and where it's earmarked to go out.

So what happens when there is unexpected money—the twenty left in the jacket pocket or the unexpected bonus and the like? As we discussed under Principle 1, what the research shows is that unless we're careful, we can blow through found money at an unbelievable rate. Because it's not earmarked for meeting any of our pre-existing goals, the found money is free to be spent on whatever short-term needs and desires may arise. Journalist Gary Belsky's book *Why Smart People Make Big Money Mistakes and How to Correct Them* has a tremendous level of additional data and analysis supporting this.

This phenomenon is why a business acquaintance of mine, who works with business owners going through liquidity events, recommends they not spend or invest any of the proceeds from the event for at least six months afterward. Their mind and mental accounting needs time to adapt to the new financial realities.

The second portion of this principle relates to a phenomenon that a close friend and I have observed: we all have certain categories we'll spend money on (even above and beyond our mental accounting estimates) with almost zero additional thought. For my wife and I, that category is dining out, almost reflexively. As major foodies living in a city like Nashville, with a great dining scene, the dining-out portion of our budget is where we generally struggle the most with keeping the spending reigned into a sensible level.

As such, in our mental accounting, we have categories where we are subconsciously cooking the books. We do not process the spending the same way we do other categories, and can be effectively blind to the spending.

PRINCIPLE 7

Wealth Is Always Defined in Comparison with Peers'

Principle 7 is near and dear to my heart because it's one in which I've most often seen friends and clients get led astray—the relative nature of wealth and spending. How we feel and consequently think about our wealth are disproportionately impacted by the people we surround ourselves with.

This has been illustrated in a few interesting ways. In the work of Firebaugh and Tach, researchers found people tend to compare themselves to peers of the same age and that relative income is more important than absolute income.[2] Researchers at the University of Warwick further added that happiness is influenced by your perception of

2 Firebaugh and Tach, "Relative Income and Happiness: Are Americans on a Hedonic Treadmill?" http://www.medicalnewstoday.com/releases/29109.php

being more highly paid than those in your social circles.[3] Fidelity in a survey of wealthy investors noted that four of ten millionaires do not feel wealthy and do not feel that way until they have $7.5 million of assets.[4]

The clear takeaway here is that when we allow our peer set to adjust as our wealth increases, we actually do ourselves a great disservice and increase our own levels of dissatisfaction with our quality of life and enjoyment.

3 https://www.sciencedaily.com/releases/2010/03/100322092057.htm
4 http://abcnews.go.com/Business/ten-millionaires-feel-wealthy-fidelity-survey-americas-richest/story?id=13132394

CHAPTER 5

COMING INTO WEALTH

"Love and work...work and love, that's all there is."

—SIGMUND FREUD

———

Where wealth comes from matters—as our brief exploration of the psychology of found money highlighted. To this point in the book, we have considered the structural elements of wealth. Now we begin to shift to something deeper, which we are calling *wealth identity*. Identity goes to something closer to the core of our conception of ourselves as humans. To begin this section, let's consider more deeply the two primary sources of wealth—event-based and work-based occurrences—and the implications of each. These implications may be either explicit or implicit in terms of how we think/respond/act in regard to our wealth.

First, we look at work and how it leads to wealth. Not only is this the most common pathway, even for those who have large liquidity events, it's also likely the work of starting and building a company that was the genesis of the wealth. That said, it seems hard to overstate the importance of work in life. Freud hit on this well when he called out love and work as the two important tasks required to build a meaningful life. Thus, it seems reasonable to consider where work fits within the broader context of wealth. For many, work is the primary method by which wealth is accumulated. Yet even for those for whom work may not be a necessity, it's a way to fill the days meaningfully.

All of us on planet Earth operate with 168 hours per calendar week. The majority of this time is spent in the following ways:

- sleep – 33 percent (If this isn't an adequate justification for never tolerating an uncomfortable mattress, I don't know what is.)
- work – 24 percent
- weekend – 17 percent
- watching TV – 13 percent (the average American watches 4.5 hours of TV per day—breathtaking, I know)
- eating – 6 percent
- getting dressed – 4 percent
- religious practice – 2 percent

Here is the rub: the single greatest thing we do in our waking hours is our work. We will spend more time at it than anything else over the course of our lives. What we do in our work matters. Moreover, if work is no longer a financial necessity, then we'll need to get creative in finding purposeful ways to fill our days.

In our considerations of wealth, it's important to acknowledge the role that work plays within it. Moreover, even as overall levels of wealth continue to increase, I believe there is an important case to be made that work should continue, and that purposeful living includes work, not a life of perpetual leisure.

Let's consider a few matters regarding work:

→ the messages we hear about work
→ the myths/falsehoods that underlie those messages
→ how we find meaningful work
→ some sticky issues relating to work

Messages We Hear About Work

What have you heard about your work, why it matters, and what you're supposed to do with it? We receive a lot of mixed messages about work. Some see work as the defining feature of their lives. Some view it as a calling. Others are quick to say that work must be about passion for it to have meaning. Some see work as a means to an end—whether it's working hard for the weekend, or working to support other interests. Many still may view work as the enemy that gets in the way of real life; others may see work as somehow tied to the baser, worldly realm, something that should be indulged only to fund the pursuit of greater, spiritual things.

There are likely many other views of work we could mention. I imagine that our own past experiences likely shape and alter our view of work as well. A workaholic father taints the view of a profession, as does the family stuck in a cycle of poverty, one that can't ever seem to catch a break.

Myths/Falsehoods that Underlie the Messages

Ultimately, behind work messages are various competing views of reality, myths we tell ourselves either consciously or unconsciously about how we make sense of the world.

One major group of messages preaches an almost Platonic view of the world. In this world, the physical world is separate from the life of the mind, or spiritual world. Work done with the hands is viewed negatively, whereas the life of the mind is exalted. This pattern of thought has certainly been a part of Western society. The American economist Thorstein Veblen was quick to highlight this in 1899 in his book *Theory of the Leisure Class*, which outlined that only certain occupations were acceptable for those of the upper class to engage in. This attitude can also be interpreted to mean that work in itself has no value and is best suited as a tool for another, more ultimate purpose in life.

Another group of messages views work as fundamentally neutral—neither good nor bad. Another group views work as everything. For many of us, how we view our work is supported by something deeper—fear. Work becomes the tool by which we counter our own deep-seated fears and anxieties about our capacity to navigate the world and the relative level and significance of our own abilities.

What We Know to Be True

Despite these varying views, there are several things we can assert to be true about work.

First, work is highly important to us, and without meaningful work, we're somehow less human. Conversely, work that's not bounded can become soul-crushing. Even if we do not need the money from work to survive, we need the work itself to survive and live fully human lives.

Second, we enjoy work more when we're better at it. Some may call this the craftsman ethos. When we are learning something new, it can be frustrating and challenging. But as we hone our skills, the work becomes more and more enjoyable.

Third, work is fundamentally creative. Work is how we take something deep within us and bring it to fruition. We can imagine the impossible or see something that did not exist before and make it real. Arguably this is true regardless of the nature of the work. Even the assembly line can be a place of great creativity for change and improvement. One way to interpret the Toyota production system and other continuous-improvement practices in manufacturing is that they finally provided a conduit for the blue-collar worker to express her innate creativity.

Finally, work can bring great joy. There are few things as wonderful, as hard, but ultimately as fulfilling as a day of work. One thinks here of the scene in film *The Shawshank Redemption* when Andy, Red, and the other prisoners retar the rooftop of the prison. After a long hard day at work, they're able to stop and drink a cold beer and admire their work. As Morgan Freeman's character remarks, "We sat and drank with the sun on our shoulders and felt like free men. Hell, we could have been tarring the roof of one of our own houses. We were the Lords of all Creation."

Meaningful Work

As we progress through life, work will be a key component of it, even if our financial resources remove the economic necessity of doing so. So how do we bring meaning to this most essential activity?

The most modern of notions is that "if you work doing what you love, you'll never work another day in your life." This sounds like such common sense; it is almost impossible to disagree with such a statement. But is the idea, in fact, helpful? Does this sentiment, in fact, offer us anything as we all search for and engage in meaningful work?

The idea of passion's centrality in determining work is most famously represented by Steve Jobs's commencement address at Stanford in 2005. Much like countless others that year, this commencement speech exhorted the new college graduates to pursue greatness and to live boldly.

And though 99 percent of addresses that year went unremembered and ultimately forgotten, this speech went viral. In fact, I'm willing to bet that many of you have seen Steve Jobs's famed Stanford address. Read again Steve's words: "You've got to find what you love. Your work is going to fill a large part of your life, and the only way to be truly satisfied is to do what you believe is great work. And the only way to do great work is to love what you do. If you haven't found it yet, keep looking. Don't settle."

I would argue that Steve's commencement address, which is wonderful to listen to, gets *almost* all the way there, he just does not stick the landing. So what did Jobs say that was helpful to how we should think about work? He tells three stories in his talk. First, he tells the story about dropping out of Reed College. The cost was too high for his working-class parents, and since he had no idea what he wanted to do with his life and wasn't sure how college would help, continuing made no sense.

What a refreshing approach to college education. Rather than wasting an inordinate amount of money—and, more important, time—chasing a degree, Jobs hit the pause button. In our modern society of rampant and runaway education inflation, it seems foolhardy to send eighteen-year-olds off to college without a clear sense of direction and sense of self. A gap year to work, learn, and mature would do wonders for many a listless college freshman.

Jobs concluded that what he did in this period in his life was only to follow his curiosity and intuition, knowing that it's simply *impossible to connect the dots looking forward.* In our worlds, which seem strangely controllable, we're quick to forget that very little of life occurs in a purely linear fashion. Someone begins school, hoping to be a marine biologist, and forty years later is a successful financial advisor. Or in Jobs's case, a deadbeat, hippy college dropout ends up founding and leading one of the most successful companies of all time. As Jobs remarked, "You have to trust the dots will connect in your future. This will give you confidence to follow your heart even when it leads you off the well-worn path."

The second key point Jobs made in his address had to do with facing failure after he was fired at the age of thirty from the company he founded. Whether it's from reading the Isaacson biography of Jobs or watching Ashton Kutcher's portrayal of him—though this may be controversial to say—Jobs deserved to be fired. He was petty, divisive, and in no capacity ready to lead a company. Where he was at his finest was as a project leader. Without his departure from Apple, I think it's clear that he would not have been able to return to Apple as the man that he did.

So how did he handle this public failure? He started over—even though he had lost the chance to do what he loved and had been blessed to do so early in life. This is a key weakness of the passion argument for career success. Life happens and gets in the way. Sometimes the ground ball takes a bad bounce and hits us in the teeth.

Yet looking back on this period in his own life, Jobs remarked that the "heaviness of success was replaced by the lightness of being a beginner again." From a place of uncertainty, he entered a period of tremendous creativity, founding both Pixar and Next.

Conan O'Brien, the late night comedian, gave a commencement speech at Dartmouth in 2011. Conan, at the time, was still recovering from his short-lived stint as the host of *The Tonight Show*. Consider how Conan reflected on this dark period in his life:

- "Disappointment stings and for driven, successful people like yourselves, it's disorienting."
- "There are few things more liberating in this life than having your worst fear realized."
- "One's dream is constantly evolving, rising and falling, changing course."
- "It is our failure to become our perceived ideal that ultimately defines us and makes us unique. It's not easy, but if you accept your misfortune and handle them right, your perceived failure can be a catalyst for profound reinvention."
- "No specific job or career goal defines me and it should not define you."

Although the two great certainties of life are death and taxes, failure and disappointment should likely be included in that category. Jobs went on to make comments about passion, but I think he misinterprets his own message. I highly doubt that the day he walked out of Apple the first time that he felt passionate about animated motion pictures. Instead, what he walked out with was a keen sense of self and a willingness to try something new.

Finally, Jobs concludes his remarks by looking at the certainty of death. He notes that remembering the certainty of death helps us make the tough choices. The fact that we all end in the same place should give us the courage to press on.

So is passion the key ingredient for professional success? I would argue that passion is not enough. What if you don't know what you love? What if your love is not financially viable? Does this mean you can't have meaningful work? Absolutely not.

Consider a few other problems with the passion hypothesis. First, there are only a select few who are extremely passionate about what they want to do from a young age. Second, where does passion come from? Arguably, passion generally is an output of mastery. The better we get at something, the more passionate we are about it. If you don't know what you're passionate about, find a place where you can do work that uses the gifts you're best at.

If your passion is not financially viable, what you're good at is needed somewhere by someone who will pay you a living wage for it. Your goal is to achieve such mastery that you can gain greater autonomy and leeway to engage in your primary desire. That may mean turning down promotions and working part time at a higher rate, etc.

Author and Georgetown professor Cal Newport has meaningfully shaped my thinking on this topic of work. His book *So Good They Can't Ignore You* is a must-read in my view in developing a career. Newport notes in his book that psychological research indicates that autonomy (the ability to work independently), competence (with skill at your job), and relatedness (in a community) are three key measures for meaningful work.

Rather than search for passion, Newport argues that what's needed is a craftsman mindset, where each person takes the skill they uniquely can offer to the world and develops it to such a degree that it allows them to have autonomy and relatedness. Becoming highly skilled at something unique and valuable sets the stage for success.

What Are the Signs of Having Found Fulfilling Work?

First, we must realize that the meaning we bring to our work, the sense of identity, the sense of fulfillment, in fact, can never be answered entirely by work itself. Work is simply work. We must accept it on its own terms and not ask more of it than it can provide. Questions of security and ultimate significance are matters far too weighty for work itself. These questions, with which we all wrestle, are nothing more than an inward struggle to find God himself.

That said, there are a few dashboard indicators we can monitor that point us in the right direction:

→ Our work is consistent with our giftedness. We're not required to engage in tasks that are beyond our level of giftedness. As Pastor Tim Keller of Redeemer Church in New York City has noted, "We must use our talents in as competent a manner as possible." This doesn't mean we shouldn't push ourselves for mastery but simply that we should not try to place a square peg in a round hole.

→ Work should be useful. Work should be ultimately about serving others and meeting a need. Deliberately impoverishing others or making communities worse off would be inconsistent with meaningful work.

→ We have other interests outside of work. We should have multiple bottom lines in life. This keeps work within its appropriate boundaries. It doesn't mean that we won't miss the kid's soccer game occasionally, but in the broad arch of life, our children will know who we are.

A Note on Professional Dreams

Is having a vision for your work the same as having a career dream? *Vision* and *dream* are not often used as synonyms, except perhaps when vision is used to describe someone having a quasimystical experience, like a prophet. Yet dreams are highly commonplace within the discussions and common parlance in our work life.

One hears of the actress who has dreamed since a young age of seeing her name on the movie theater marquee. Or of the musician who dreams of being the next great rock-and-roll artist. When children express these dreams, we look at them indulgently, if not condescendingly, because dreams of this sort often seem like the most common usage of dreams, what our brains do when we sleep. Dreams of this sort are fuzzy around the edges, but for most, they don't generally result in serious life change.

Yet, for a very few, those dreams translate into life change. That same struggling actress picks up and moves to Los Angeles. The musician comes to Nashville to write songs and sing in honky-tonk bars. For the vast majority, those dreams will ultimately prove to be as ethereal as their nighttime brethren.

They won't be discovered by the big-name producer. Although a steady stream of work starring in toothpaste commercials provides a modicum of a paycheck, it never translates into a box-office berth. Or perhaps they just aren't talented enough relative to the highly competitive ranks of others seeking to do the same. Clearly, it's highly likely that the longer-term contemplation of one's career—and, daresay, one's dreams—is likely to involve the heartbreak of the dream not coming true.

For myself, this has been a true tale. In the fall of my senior year of college, a family friend who was a financial advisor gave me a book—Roger Lowenstein's biography of Warren Buffet. As the son and grandson of doctors, this was my first encounter with the investing world and the stock markets, and I was instantly hooked. From that point on, for the next ten years, I worked tirelessly on Wall Street, hoping to become an investor, chasing my own dream of investment success.

This ultimately culminated in my starting an investment partnership, similar to the original Buffett Partnership of the 1950s. After four years, the partnership failed to take root. In the aftermath of closing the business, the loss was extremely painful. I've often wrestled deeply with my prior dream. Was I wrong to have it in the first place? And now that it's gone, do I dare create a new one?

In considering all this, I've somewhat settled on the following view. Considering my career in light of skills/autonomy/bigger purpose is relevant even after the end of a dream. Understanding my own skill set and then seeking to place that on the right platform is a core dynamic that can remain consistent as dreams come and go.

The Side Effect of Work: Wealth Accumulation

I recognize that many of my comments in these last few pages are philosophical in tone, but because of the importance of work, it would be incomplete to discuss its primary side effect—that is, the generation of wealth—without considering the thing in itself. There is an old saying that someone goes bankrupt slowly and quickly. The steady accumulation of bad choices leads to a sudden break. The inverse is true generally for the most common mode of wealth accumulation. As a person ages into a career, higher levels of disposable income, performance-based compensation, and other opportunities come along that begin to build the engine for wealth creation.

Although this book focuses on the transition points when wealth has accumulated to such a point that it affects behavior, work to some degree will likely be involved in that. As such, it's important to understand the various ways that wealth is accumulated through work, as well as the various, risks, rewards, features, and benefits of each.

I've found several primary paths by which work generates wealth:

- ➤ salaried professional
- ➤ C-suite executive
- ➤ recurring-book-of-business professional
- ➤ eat-what-you-kill sales producer
- ➤ artist
- ➤ entrepreneur

After discussing each path, we will outline key components for the capital each type generates.

The Salaried Professional

Consider a hypothetical *Joe Smith*, Vice President of Accounting at any given Fortune 500 company. The salaried professional is probably what most quickly comes to mind when one considers the upper-middle class, but maybe not the wealthy. Like IBM executives of old, with a navy blue suit and white shirt, the image that comes to mind of the salaried professional is one of slow and steady progression toward a goal. Within large corporate enterprises, these executives report for work dutifully each day. With the passage of time, the right level of political savvy and solid work, upward mobility awaits. A typical career path progresses along the lines of functional operator, team manager, functional manager, division head, and potentially the C-suite. At each level, there are well-known and defined benchmarks of compensation and incentive awards through equity and bonus programs.

What are the key considerations for the various forms of capital such an individual possesses? Financial capital is generally high income but with low upside—meaning total compensation is relatively well known. And in a mature industry, it's unlikely that an IPO or other event is going to provide a large one-time boost to net income. This means that investments assets are accumulated generally through steady savings and ongoing market returns. The primary financial risk is that consumption (given the high levels of incoming cash flow) consistently and regularly diverts capital from flowing through to investments.

From an intellectual capital perspective, job tenure certainly is not what it used to be. In a prior era, the expectation of lifetime employment was not unreasonable, and, as such, getting the right degree/credential required to get the first job was the most important move. In today's market, it's not unreasonable to consider that some degree of ongoing human capital investment will be required to add new skills as technology makes your existing skill set obsolete. In all likelihood, the economic cost of this investment may be shared by the employer via corporate training (in-house corporate universities). Arguably, corporate professionals need to be their own quarterback, reading the tea leaves to determine what skills are likely to be needed in the future and then finding ways to source them.

Community and connectedness remain paramount in the modern era. Study after study has consistently identified that soft connections are the primary pathway by which job opportunities are filled. Developing and maintaining broad networks of relationships serve a vitally important function in filling these roles. They keep career options available in the event of a career stall, an unruly superior, or bad luck.

The C-Suite Executive

The career salaried professional represents a separate, subsegment that's worth exploring in some detail—the C-suite executive of a public company. First let's compare the peak of someone's career in other professional fields versus those working for public companies. For a physician, depending on whether in private practice, a large hospital system, or in an academic setting, there is a natural transition that occurs when the physician goes from employee to partner, or employee to department head, etc. This stage may be accompanied by additional professional responsibilities and/ or investment into becoming an owner of the professional corporation. Those in a hospital system or academic setting may become chair of the department or head of Neurology, etc.

Accompanying this increase in title may be an increase in salary and, as I mentioned, an equity component. But generally the partnership agreement dictates when/how this ownership is distributed in the event that the partner wishes to retire or make a professional change. In the case of private practice, the ownership interest becomes a de facto way to acquire access to a larger cash flow stream (that is, partner distribution above and beyond the annual salary component). Although this ownership piece has some residual value at the end of a career, it's unlikely to become a sizable piece of someone's net worth, where it carries a disproportionate weighting.

The same is true for partners in a law, accounting, or consulting firm. The partnership interest represents incremental cash flow with some value at the end of the career. From a financial capital perspective, handling this transition is largely consistent with how the salary inflow has been managed before—by working to find a balance between asset accumulation and consumption.

The C-suite executive, and especially the chief executive officer, has a markedly different occurrence. In my experience reviewing the executive compensation disclosures filed in the proxy statements of several hundred different public companies, there are some commonalities to how the compensation packages are structured. Typically, there is a base-salary component and an annual cash-compensation piece that represents a percentage of base. In my opinion, despite often 50 percent or more of total annual compensation being at risk through a performance-related bonus, the annual package component functions similarly to those of other senior professionals generating high annual cash flows.

The difference is in the equity-compensation piece. Starting often at the vice-president levels, through the use of stock options and restricted stock, ownership is used as a way to align employee behavior with the company interests. Known as the principal/agent problem, the news headlines are replete with stories of public company management teams using corporate resources to enrich themselves at the expense of shareholders. In theory, by creating alignment between the two, and with a stock price representing the discounted present value of future cash flows, by disproportionately weighting someone's net worth toward that figure, you create alignment of interest. What does that mean from a wealth-strategy perspective? A number of things come to mind.

First, huge concentration risk. By the time you reach the C-suite, it's not unreasonable to expect that 60-70 percent of someone's net worth is exposed to the value of the company stock. As we all saw with the employees of En-ron and Lehman Brothers, that sort of concentration risk can be dangerous—especially in highly levered, cyclical companies. This seems like something corporate compensation committees would recognize—that a disproportionate weighting of someone's net worth can actually result in poor management by discouraging long-term thinking and the sort of risk taking required to continue to drive corporate results in the long term.

Second, cost-basis issues. Large option packages/compensation arrangements may have been accumulated over the course of a long employment with the same company. As such, many of the shares may be at an initial price or cost basis that's so low that they become in effect almost unsalable due to the tax gains incurred on the sale.

Third, psychological biases. Being in control of or helping to manage a company can result in a lack of objectivity about the company's prospects and longer-term risks. Even after leaving, it's easy to view the company through rose-colored lenses that affect objectivity of consideration. These issues require a long-term and in-depth plan to manage the risks as well as capture opportunities.

What other constraints accompany the C-suite executive? In terms of intellectual capital, time demands and pressures may prohibit the individual from cultivating new skills or other interests. Social capital and engagement likely shift to board-focused roles where nonprofit boards are seeking the support of the larger corporate parent and access to a possible corporate foundation or resources.

For-profit board roles may begin to open up as well. These can provide a nice diversification of income, since many provide annual cash and stock compensation.

The Recurring-Book-of-Business Professional

Another subsegment of working professionals who go on to generally accumulate sizable financial wealth are what I call *book-of-business professionals*. These professionals sell a service/product that effectively renews annually. A common example would be insurance salespeople who generate a portfolio of policies that renew each year. Financial advisors would also be an example.

Individuals with this type of earnings power to generate financial capital have a few additional nuances to consider. At first glance, this individual looks a lot like any entrepreneur—with a lot of potential and possibly a good idea, but little to show for it. From a financial-assets perspective, their earnings potential is extremely high risk, closer to a biotechnology stock with a single product that's either going to work or not. From an overall-assets perspective, because of the volatility of the initial capital, it seems highly prudent that these professionals maintain a large cash balance at the outset and or a lot of low-risk bonds to mitigate the risk from an overall portfolio perspective.

Overtime, as the book of business accumulates, the sticky nature of the client base and line of sight to each year's revenue implies that the bond-portion of the portfolio more or less migrates away from the financial assets to the nature of the earnings power. Depending on the nature of the book of business, it's important to *beta* adjust the stream of earnings generating the annual cash flow to make sure that it's treated with the right risk mindset. In non-financial speak, we must consider how volatile the renewal rates of the product are. For example, for a financial advisor, industry averages point to client retention of roughly 98 percent annually. So this earnings stream is exceptionally stable. Conversely though, increasingly the dominant way of being paid in the industry is through a fixed percentage of assets under management.

By being invested in the capital markets, the underlying assets that support this assets-under-management charge for the advisor are exposed to the volatility of both stocks and bonds. Thankfully, because clients, and moreover the aggregate portfolio of firm assets, are not investing entirely in equities, it's unlikely to see a total peak-to-trough drawdown as significant as the equity market. A simple 50/50 portfolio saw a mid-twenties rate of decline during the global financial crisis of 2008-2009. It's also worth highlighting that professional services firms with these book-of-business characteristics predominantly have cost structures composed of employees. As such, during periods of volatile earnings, the business can see sizable losses in bad times if the firm allows its infrastructure to run too far ahead of a sober assessment of the business's cash-flow-generation potential that takes into account both the good times and the bad.

As we consider constraints on wealth strategy, the book-of-business professional is unique both in the annual renewal characteristics of the business (which overtime results in an earnings profile that looks more bondlike—or even similar to that of a tenured college professor). This analogy does not entirely hold true, given some embedded liability due to underlying economic cycle sensitivity.

The Eat-What-You-Kill Sales Producer

The commission-based sales professional is the closest thing to a purely economic animal in modern economic times. Each year, come January first, the slate is wiped clean and the quota resets. Although, over time, the salesperson hopes to build a client base that can bring in revenue with some degree of predictability, that may not necessarily be the case.

Even a great residential/commercial real estate broker starts the year generally not knowing who will be the most significant client of the year. Senior investment bankers, especially at sell-side M&A boutiques, which may operate on a purely contingency-fee basis, are similar to this.

So what are unique considerations for these professionals? First, what instinctively comes to mind here is the volatility of the earnings potential. It's important to balance this with cash and lower-risk fixed-income investments.

Strategic risk: making sure that what's being sold still has a market—that is, no one wants to become the best buggy whip salesperson.

Stasis/air-pocket risk: Many folks need transactions, either because times are good and they want to buy assets or because times are bad and the credit cycle/bankruptcy concerns will force activity. But in the interim period, like a plane following a parabolic flight path, there can be a period of weightlessness where there is simply no market for assets. Survivability is key.

The Artist

Calling Nashville home, I have been fortunate to spend time with a number of folks in the music business. Spending time with such artists has led to a lot of thinking and analysis about how creatives should think about their financial capital.

I want to look at the course of a songwriter's career, how their earnings move, and how they should think about investing as a result. We're using songwriters as an example, but these considerations should be relevant to any successful creative artist.

So starting out, the creative leaves home/college and most likely moves to Nashville or Los Angeles to begin the process of building a career. They are in coffee shops, meeting other writers, and having writing sessions. Perhaps, most likely, they're working a side hustle or two to bring in cash flow. Times are lean and mean.

This period is transformative because they're starting with a dream but are uncertain as to what income stream the dream will produce. To my mind, this seems a lot like an oil company leasing a plot of land. They think there may be oil to be extracted, but the exact amount and for how long are likely highly variable.

Suppose our songwriter writes a first successful song that gets moderate airplay and a little commercial success. From an investing perspective, this song is fascinating to consider, and I think continuing the oil-drilling analogy makes sense. There is a lot of hard work and cost that goes into setting up an oil well and preparing it for drilling. Once the hole is drilled and the well begins to produce, it's about realizing a return on the investment.

Taking an idea to a hit is by no means an easy feat. Yet once the song is in place and successful, it begins to produce a revenue stream for the writer. In theory, over time, this writer is going to produce a series of little oil wells that are going to produce a revenue stream. As important, though, these streams exhibit a decline curve as time passes and the song receives less airtime and generates less royalties.

From an investment perspective then, there are a couple of considerations to highlight. The first is that the way the decline curve works means that the songwriter likely continues to need to produce new product and add to the *wells* producing income.

As these wells are added to, the writer needs to capture a spread between income and expenses in the form of additional investments and savings. From an investor's perspective, our goal is to transform the songwriter's assets from a series of *oil wells* exhibiting decline curves to a steady pool of liquid assets that produce a regular stream of income. The artist needs to save enough assets so that a ~4 percent distribution rate off the assets supports a desired standard of living.

Here is the tension. The assets needed to generate a sizable pool of capital to produce the stable income stream would seem to indicate a need to have a higher allocation to equities to generate as large a return as possible. Yet the variability of when the next hit will arise (and arguably the formative lean years at the start of the career) would advocate for a lower-risk portfolio. The nature of how a songwriter generates a living is high risk, like the equity market, and so to compensate for that riskiness, the investment assets should be more in bonds. How do we reconcile this tension? Keep the standard of living low for as long as possible to allow capital to accumulate as fast as possible.

The Entrepreneur

Entrepreneurs are unique in that they are a hybrid of several types we've already discussed. When the entrepreneur launches a new venture, the zero-to-one moment, to use American entrepreneur Peter Thiel's term, they are a case study of concentration. They have concentrated the entirety of their human/intellectual capital in an idea. Having started four companies personally, the months and sometimes years leading up to the launch of a new venture are a dynamic and thrilling time where every effort is focused entirely on bringing the new venture to fruition. A college professor, and friend of mine, said in his entrepreneurship class in college that entrepreneurs are often perceived in the press as being those that bear risk. The point being that when someone goes through the process of starting a new venture, they are doing something incredibly risky.

My professor argued instead that what great entrepreneurs do is the exact opposite. They work acutely to minimize or remove risks, so that by the time the business launches, they hope they've handicapped the risks to such a degree that they're bearable—relative to the potential reward available if the venture turns out to be successful. The launch and early stage period are about the assessment and management of this de-risk/risk-structuring process.

Of course, nearly all entrepreneurs make a sizable financial commitment to the venture. They may plunge the entirety of their life savings, leave well-paying prestigious careers and the like in order to pursue their dreams. Like the human-capital element, the entrepreneur has meaningful concentration in their financial assets as well.

And then the business takes off. For the purposes of this analysis, let's exclude the unique subset of new ventures, the rapidly growing unicorns and the like. Instead, like many successful ventures, this business begins to grow and grow a bit over time.

As the business scales, the entrepreneur hopes to go from paying himself no salary to most likely a modest one, focusing instead on plowing profits from the company back into the company. The entrepreneur defers the gratification of near-term cash upside in exchange for the higher growth potential being offered.

So in terms of an accumulation pathway toward financial rewards, the entrepreneur looks like our artist, our senior executive, and our sales professional in their earnings. They are like the artist because they're creating something out of nothing and hoping there is a market for it. Like the sales professional, the entrepreneurs hustle aggressively to bring in every dollar once the business is up and running, knowing that unless they sell, there won't be a paycheck. And ultimately, once the business is in place, entrepreneurs wrestle to define the correct ratio of profit to take today versus the level of profit to reinvest. The net result of this deliberation is hoped to be a regular salary that must be saved against accumulating some additional financial assets that are separate from the business.

Like the successful executive, through balanced living without consumption beyond one's means, entrepreneurs, now executives at their own company, likely begin to work toward accumulating a pool of assets to diversify the excessive levels of concentration risk that have brought them to this point.

Knowing all this, what should the entrepreneur keep in mind during the progression of the business? First, at the start, it's worth attempting to keep in mind a reasonable expectation of the base rate of failure for similar ventures. This helps to accurately handicap the level of personal investment along with the length of time one might be willing to stay invested in the venture. Second, keep an open, skeptical mind. If at any point you were to start the business again with the benefit of the new information gathered and you chose not to start the business or to materially alter the business itself, recognize the significance of this warning sign. We spoke earlier about the task of risk assessment, mitigation, and incurrence that the entrepreneur is conducting.

Each step in that process is about validating a hypothesis about how the business will succeed. Or perhaps better stated, knowing that you cannot ultimately prove a positive, but instead only disprove a negative, you work to disprove the negative of your positive thesis. When you surface data that is supportive of the negative thesis—for example, that this product does not fit the market—it's worth considering a possible course correction at that time.

Once the business thesis has been validated and the company becomes a going concern, the task shifts toward management of growth and funding that growth. Starving oneself and/or the company of capital is a long-run recipe for disaster. Thoughtfully structuring savings and investment programs becomes paramount as this time.

A Large Liquidity Event

Entrepreneurs are a natural transition point to our next consideration about the second pathway through which wealth is typically accumulated—the transformative liquidity event. This sort of liquidity typically comes at the end of a fairly lengthy period of time spent building a business asset. For businesses that grow very quickly—the proverbial unicorn of Silicon Valley—the next section on luck/liquidity is probably more relevant, since the element of the success is simply due to someone who managed to catch lightning.

In the more common scenario, we see the fruits of a long duration of time. It may have taken fifteen to twenty years or more of work to build the business. Thousands of hours, missed ballgames, ruined vacations, and sleepless nights are common among all who are compelled to scratch the entrepreneurial itch.

At the outset, it's worth spending time in deep consideration of the driver for the sale itself. There are likely a number of possible reasons for the transactions. Here are a few common ones:

→ *A change in the business environment.* Whether due to technological change or the merger of two primary competitors, the forces of creative destruction affect all businesses. The ever-changing landscape may mean that while your business is performing fine today, the tea leaves indicate that changes are coming and making a move earlier rather than later makes more sense.

→ *The business is struggling.* Unanticipated changes, loss of a major contract, or unmanageable debt load—whatever the reasons—the business has fallen on hard times and the best (and perhaps only) path forward is to sell the business.

→ *Succession plan is unclear.* It has been a great run building the business, but your kids don't want the rock quarry and there is no internal candidate who has demonstrated the leadership required to run the business.

→ *Establish a clear succession plan.* Your kids do want the business, and you want to help establish them as the clear leadership in the company, so you agree to sell your ownership to aid in the succession planning.

→ *There's an unforeseen crisis.* Despite their expectations to the contrary, 100 percent of businesses founders' lives end in death. At the risk of being excessively tongue in cheek, many owners do not put adequate plans in place in case the worst were to transpire. The end result being that the business is forced to transact, perhaps quickly, to help the family move on, pay estate taxes, etc.

In terms of a large liquidity event, it's important to understand the specific transformation that occurs in these circumstances. Consider life prior to the event. Most likely the business owner is paying himself some sort of a salary and receiving profit distributions from the business. The salary may be at a market rate for the size of the business, but it may even be lower to help provide some room for growth, as well as to keep the business profitable and in a place where it can continue to grow.

As a result, the owner receives profit distributions each year, which are a nice sweetener to the salary. But the distributions are far from guaranteed and move up and down with the economy and operating results of the business. Most likely, some portion of these distributions is spent to help support lifestyle expenses.

At this stage, the owner's wealth accumulation looks similar to other high-income earners. Wealth is deferred through the use of vehicles like a 401(k) plan and ongoing savings. The business certainly retains economic value and ideally continues to grow. But there is perhaps always some degree of uncertainty about the value of the business, especially given the owner's acute recollection of the times in the life of the business when it seemed that its days were doomed.

Thus, when the business ultimately transacts, the shift from illiquid capital to liquid capital is incredibly important and likely raises a whole host of other emotional issues. First, the dollar amount received in some ways signifies the value of a lifetime's work. Clinging too strongly to that specific dollar figure may have an outsized impact on whether too much or too little risk is taken when the portfolio is ultimately invested. But it's important to honor this implied value and not be hasty to immediately redeploy the capital.

Second, the movement from liquid to illiquid capital often indicates that the chances of making it again are less likely. Certainly, there are several individuals who have a demonstrated track record of repeatedly being able to build and monetize businesses. I would argue that impressive though they are, they represent a minority of business owners. Instead, the owner who transacts and realizes a healthy sum can be thought of in some ways as analogous to a retiring professional baseball player. Although some income certainly awaits in the post-retirement years, the chance at the big dollars has come and gone.

Accompanying the reality of the monetization of the business are a whole host of important and powerful emotions, such as relief, concerns about the future, and mourning/loss. All these emotions are valuable inputs in the consideration of the next phase in life and what it may hold.

Other Considerations. *What are the terms of the transaction and their impact?* Cash on the barrelhead is nice, but that's only one possible form of compensation offered during a transaction. Instead, the owner may be offered a combination of cash and stock in the new company. There may be cash up front and a note that pays off over a period of time. Often, there may be some cash today and an earn-out arrangement that offers additional compensation to encourage the management team to remain in place and continue the growth trajectory of the business.

The variety of options speaks acutely to the need for the individual prior to the liquidity event to have walked through the process we outline later in the book—understanding personal goals and the desired financial resources needed to support the thoughtful evaluation of any transaction. Before the transaction, it's important to consider the philanthropic goals as well. Through the use of donor-advised funds and other structures, it's possible to not only save material amounts of taxes during the transaction but also maximize the dollar amount given to charity.

All owners would do well to remember that terms matter vitally, and you must handicap the downside risk of continuing to own the stock. Chapter 10, "How to Invest," walks through some dynamics on this matter at much greater length. There may be other pathways to help mitigate some of this risk worth discussing in much greater detail with a sophisticated financial advisor.

So what does the path forward look like with a large liquidity event? Recognizing that survey data show that the vast majority of exiting owners are unhappy after a transaction transpires, I offer a few points that may help mitigate this.

First, avoid the pressure to make any decisions quickly. As we saw in the chapter on psychology, found money is quick to burn a hole in the pocket. Wait a healthy period of time so that your mind becomes used to the reality of your new level of liquidity.

Second, consider where/how this new wealth fits within your existing life plan and goals. Be skeptical of its potential to change your entire life plan. As Thoreau noted, "Beware of all enterprises that require new clothes." For sure, new opportunities will arise with the change in station. But, arguably, that which made you happy beforehand will be that which does so afterward. Avoid the Joneses and, more important, avoid any Jacks selling magic beans that somehow will bring more satisfaction to your life.

Third, appropriately mourn the change. Major life change unbalances and unmoors us all, no matter how grand we are. Beware the temptation to feel guilty about feeling unsettled by the notion that your newfound financial resources are somehow supposed to remove all uncertainty. The belief that wealth solves all of life's problems is something that only poor people hold to.

Fourth, when the time is right and the opportunity seems reasonable, you may consider your next venture. But avoid the temptation of believing that you're the next Warren Buffett. Sometimes the blind squirrel gets lucky. Until you've proven a repeatable process in building multiple organizations, be careful to limit the amount of personal capital you're willing to put at risk in any one deal. Making money as a business owner is dramatically different from doing so as an investor. We will cover this in greater detail in a later chapter.

Fifth, recognize the risk/uniqueness in having a large pool of cash. This is not a commonly considered constraint, but how you think about and manage your wealth will be affected by the outsized level of cash in the portfolio after the transaction closes. Laying out a thoughtful plan for deployment is critical to avoid taking too much risk too quickly. Conversely, taking too little risk can be just as damaging if you're hesitant to put any capital to work. I once met with a large, wealthy family in Greenwich, CT, which had basically been invested 80 percent in cash for five years following the financial crisis because they were waiting for market conditions to improve.

At this point, the S&P was up over 200 percent from its March 2009 lows. Although prudence relative to market risk incurred is important, there is not a bell rung at the top or bottom of the market cycle. As economist Ben Graham noted, and as I repeat often to clients, "Investing is most successful when it is most businesslike." Avoiding emotion-driven decision-making is key across the market cycles.

A transaction likely means the loss of control. This may seem self-evident, but founders who retain ownership in the new company are often likely to have too much concentration risk to the acquired firm, believing that they're still able to effect change and exercise control of the destiny of the firm. Soberly assessing the actual level of control is a necessary input to determining how much concentration risk you're willing to take with your new employer.

The Lucky and the Inheritor

There is a second type of liquidity event that is dramatically different from that experienced by the builder of a business. The lucky, such as lottery winners, and their close cousins, the inheritors, are probably the most envied, and least understood among the rich.

The innate attraction to these figures is simply a result of the great ease with which their station in life was attained. In considering job paths to this point, we've had the common threads of capital accumulation, years and years of advanced education and training, long hours in building a business, hustling for sales, etc. Although perhaps not as grimy as the jobs television host Mike Rowe so thoroughly profiles in his show *Dirty Jobs*, they share the requirements of time/effort/sacrifice, along with a fair share of good fortune to avoid catastrophic loss that would render the effort for naught. The lucky and lucky sperm share none of these travails. Whether due to superior breeding or a two-dollar Mega Millions ticket purchased at the local gas station, they arrived at their station in life with no effort of their own.

Meet the Apologetic Owners. Although most envied and least understood, the lucky here are likely among the most isolated of wealthy segments. Consider the grandchildren of a wealthy business owner. The grandfather started the business with a dream perhaps of providing for his family and potentially building something that might last for the long-term. His life and friends were made during the course of his assent into wealth, but likely his closest of friends were around before wealth came into the picture.

His children, depending on their ages, are likely to remember portions of the climb in net worth. Their lives were likely well-to-do, but depending on the speed of growth of the business, their lifestyles perhaps were tempered by either a lack of overall liquidity or their father's own desire for them to be raised in an environment similar to the one in which he was raised.

Our story line is of course hypothetical, and likely the experiences of what we're calling the lucky are tempered by their own family's history. Regardless, the case is that at some point, there will be a generation that arises that is simply unaware of life before wealth. As this section's title indicates, these owners are often apologetic for their balance sheet largess, since they did very little to earn the resources they've acquired.

Perhaps the resources were transferred to them, maybe as a component of a thoughtful process of gifting the blessings and responsibilities of stewardship on to the next generation. More likely, the assets were transferred as an estate tax liability-management tool. What business owner wants to pay more in taxes? Accordingly, as these transfers were designed and structured to solve a prior generation's problem, they come loaded with the structures and restrictions imposed by the prior generation. It's their wealth they're passing on, and accordingly they have rights in seeing how it's used.

I pause here, of course, to acknowledge the common response to this predicament of "it must be nice" or "first-world problems" or "that's just the next generation being ungrateful." I once sat in a networking group of other advisors to high-net-worth families. When the discussion turned to the particular issues that next-generation family members face, one of the other attendees was quick with a quip that the recipients were greedy and spoiled and that's why they were having a difficulty with a structure.

Before rushing to judgment, can we observe though the uniqueness of their predicament? For the majority of inheritors, the wealth does not come outright but instead via a trust. Trusts are an important legal structure designed to ensure that property is held for the benefit of another, and their roots can be traced back to the Middle Ages.

The caveat to this is that trusts run contrary to every conception of ownership we experience during our developmental years. Say, for example, I have a seven-year-old son. Imagine for Christmas one year, instead of giving him his gift outright, we instead create the following scenario:

"Oh, Dad, thanks so much, I really wanted a new Star Wars nerf gun to play with."

"Of course, you're welcome son. It's my pleasure. You need to understand a few things first. I was worried that someone might come and try and take your gun so I did a couple things to keep it safe for you."

"Oh, so you bought like a warranty on it?" says the precocious child.

"Not really," the father continues. "The gun is yours to use, but it's not owned by you. Instead, do you remember Mr. Haskel, whom I play golf with? Mr. Haskel has agreed to oversee the gun. Whenever you want to use it, all you have to do is ask Mr. Haskel for the gun and he will let you play with it."

"Okay. Do I have to give it back when I'm done?"

"Yes. Mr. Haskel's job is to take care of the gun and make sure it's well used. So anytime you're done with it, you just bring it back to him. He'll keep it maintained and working. And I've given him a few instructions about what I think it looks like to have a healthy amount of fun with the gun. After all, we wouldn't want your new toys getting in the way of schoolwork, now would we?"

We'll end our scene there. Of course, you can see the tension in this ridiculous thought experiment of ours but it's absurd on a deeper level as well. No matter how well drafted the documents are, the experience of having an asset in trust is very different from the ownership relationship we experience when we own something outright.

This is why Jay Hughes notes from his experience in working with wealthy families that 80 percent of those with a trust fund view it as an unbeneficial influence in their lives. So the inheritor experiences some of the benefits and responsibilities of wealth, but in a manner unique within the economy. As Jamie Johnson, of the Johnson and Johnson family, observed in his excellent documentary *Born Rich*, "I live outside the American dream. That was something my grandfather did. Now I have to build my own meaningful life."

So in considering the things that constrain or impair our ability to think strategically about wealth, being an inheritor brings several to mind:

→ **Difference in type of ownership and ability to exercise control.** We've already covered this concept, looking at the difference between ownership and being the beneficiary of an instrument that is in fact the owner. This tension becomes more interesting when we consider it in light of research that indicates that autonomy, mastery, and purpose are keys to purposeful work.

Author Daniel Pink covered this at length in his book *Drive* and in his TED Talk on the same subject. Being a beneficiary is in fact antithetical to autonomy because it makes your dreams and desires always subject to the intervention of another party. This tension is worth deep consideration by those who are beneficiaries, as well as those asked to serve in the capacity of trustee.

→ **Constrained by isolation.** Because their wealth and often even their last names isolate them from the general public, inheritors can also be the loneliest of our wealthy cohorts. Their loneliness is perhaps rivaled only by the loneliness of the extremely famous celebrity.

This separation and isolation manifests itself in many ways. First, there is likely always a degree of suspicion in relationships, whether or not the relationship exists only because of the presence of assets. This suspicion makes trust difficult at best and impossible at worst.

Even the very environment in which inheritors are raised can serve as a constraint on their interaction with wealth. First, let's consider the benefits of money in its simplest form. As a store of value, money facilitates the ease of exchange of goods and services. Those raised with exceptionally high level of wealth are uniquely positioned to make nearly all exchanges. It sounds fundamentally obvious to say that the wealthy are able to buy what they wish, but consider the impact of this reality. Without limits on affordability, one can consume at will. The individual in these circumstances is faced with an excessive number of choices.

As psychologist Barry Schwartz notes in *The Paradox of Choice*, having more choices is not necessarily always in someone's best interest. In fact, being limited in choosing can actually be a net benefit to someone's happiness. This excessive level of choice often manifests itself in individuals who are unable to narrow a vocation because they cannot decide where to begin. Too many choices and no economic imperative to work undermine the person's ability to exercise self-determination.

Much ink has been spilled about the potential issues of lifestyle. I do not think there is much more to be added about the dangers of lifestyles of excessive consumption or hedonism. Instead, it's worth highlighting the impact that prior generations can have on those that come after by not providing restraints on spending.

Whether it's due to not wanting to be seen as a buzz kill by restraining their kids or the concern over the family's reputation, we can do irreparable harm by not providing limits. I'm reminded here of a story I heard of one first generation wealth creator saying, "No grandchild of mine is going to be in a third-story walk-up railroad apartment. That's not how [insert wealthy family's name] live." Accordingly, this kind grandfather then proceeds to give his grandchild a monthly allowance for housing, which robs her of the ability to self-determine, choose a vocation, or receive the economic rewards commensurate with its standing.

As we mentioned earlier, the lucky find themselves in similar shoes. The lottery winner and the like find themselves in circumstances they did not plan. The feelings of tension, isolation, and concern are only more concentrated and magnified for the lucky.

Whatever the reason driving the transaction, the large liquidity event can transform your financial resources and potentially large portions of life itself. Carefully evaluating those possible impacts and putting guardrails in place allow the day after the transaction to be a pleasant and less-disconcerting one.

Questions to Consider

➤ How does the amount of wealth I am to receive compare to my notion of what it means to be financially wealthy?

Books to Consider

There have been some phenomenal resources written on the subject of work. A few reference guides that I would commend to you include:

What Color Is Your Parachute, Richard Bolles

Never Eat Alone, Keith Ferrazzi

So Good They Can't Ignore You, Cal Newport

How Will You Measure Your Life?, Clayton Christensen

Books on Inheritance

Raised Healthy, Wealthy and Wise: Lessons from Successful and Grounded Inheritors on How They Got That Way, Coventry Edwards-Pitt

Silver Spoon Kids: How Successful Parents Raise Responsible Kids, Eileen Gallo

Cycle of the Gift: Family Wealth and Wisdom, James Hughes, Susan Massenzio, and Keith Whitaker

Navigating the Dark Side of Wealth: A Life Guide for Inheritors, Thayer Cheatham Willis

Born Rich (a documentary), Jamie Johnson

SECTION TWO

WEALTH
IDENTITY

CHAPTER 6

HOW YOU FEEL ABOUT YOURSELF AFFECTS HOW YOU FEEL ABOUT WEALTH

"Where are the guideposts or roadmaps for someone for whom the question is not, "How do I make a living?" but rather, "Given that I have money, how do I live well?"

—KEITH WHITAKER, *FAMILY TRUSTS*

———

Before you can understand your relationship to wealth, you must know who you are. So let's begin by first considering the simplest and greatest question of life: Who am I? Cherie Herder, who runs the Trinity Forum, a D.C.-based think tank that helps spur "thinking leaders to interact with leading thinkers," tells us that there are three great questions in life that we must answer: What is the good life? What is a good person? And what is the just society?

The second and third questions, while thought provoking and timely for us all, are beyond the scope of this discussion and are likely best answered in a community of others and under the guidance of your personal religious practice. Nevertheless, the answer to those two questions will have a tremendous impact on how your wealth is managed.

For now, let's wrestle with the first question: What is the good life? We live in a fast-paced, pragmatic world and taking the time for deep contemplation/consideration of concerns of our own identity often feels tedious, at best, and quaint and dated at worst. But let me offer some tools for getting started.

One of my favorite movies is *The Emperor's Club,* starring Kevin Klein, who plays an inspirational teacher working at a prestigious boarding school. Through lessons of history and the classics, Klein's character, Mr. Hundert, seeks to impart an ethic and standard of living befitting these young men, who are destined for greatness. Mr. Hundert takes seriously his role and responsibility in the development of the philosopher kings of tomorrow. This all comes to a head, of course, when the world of theory comes face to face with the world of fact, as the philosophical Hundert meets Sedgwick Bell, a functional Machiavellian with a bit of German philosopher Friedrich Nietzsche's *Will to Power* sprinkled in for good measure.

Their encounter is germane to our consideration of wealth in that we all tend to act a bit more like Mr. Bell than Mr. Hundert, that is, we're pragmatists, not philosophers. Yet—having interacted extensively with the wealthy throughout my career, as well as journeying through my own path into their ranks—I believe philosophy is actually what's needed most. We would all do well to heed the warning of the Oracle of Delphi: know thyself.

Who Am I?

Understanding the self is challenging. Trying to objectively look at your own life seems nearly impossible. And there are so many moving parts and levels to each of us that it is hard to know where to begin. To help in that, I developed the Self-and-Money Framework (see Exhibit 6.1) to help you systematically consider the various elements that make up your life.

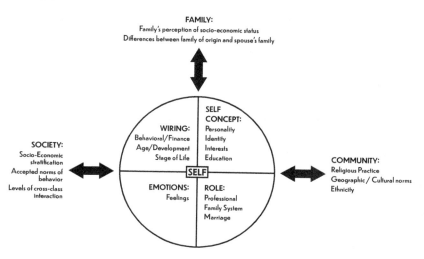

EXHIBIT 6.1 THE SELF-AND-MONEY FRAMEWORK

Let's begin with the interior circle of the diagram—considering the self. What is the self? In its simplest and most colloquial form, self is our attempt to answer the question of who and why we are. But much like a solid object, which can be further reduced to molecules, atoms, quarks, etc., the self can be broken down into further detail. It can be helpful to consider four major buckets: wiring, self-concept, emotions, and roles.

Wiring

This bucket considers the elements of who we are and is rooted in a neurological foundation. The question of how the cells in our brain actually function would rest here. As we discussed in Chapter 3, "Level of Wealth," how our brain is wired to consider financial questions is worth understanding.

Self-Concept

Understanding more deeply our own particular way of thinking of ourselves can be of real value. There are a number of different personality assessments that can provide some windows into the black box of our own psyche. None of these personality-assessment tools is flawless. That said, in my experience, if you answer the questions quickly—capturing your first blush response, not the response of the person you wish to be—they can serve as a helpful diagnostic tool. Below are outlined a few that I have found to be particularly useful in deepening the knowledge of one's self.

First and arguably the most famous of these assessments is the Myers-Briggs Type Indicator (MBTI), which works to apply Jungian psychology to the complex problem of personality. Some people have mixed feelings about the MBTI, finding that they do not clearly fall into one category. My experience was the exact opposite. My MBTI profile had me pegged cold. Although I'm becoming much more introverted the older I get, the rest of the assessment was spot on. As someone who has always struggled a bit to understand where and how I fit, the MBTI was a breath of fresh air and something I still reference to this day. MBTI, in my estimation, is helpful in understanding what and how I do many things—often subconsciously.

The second tool is the Enneagram. While it has ancient roots, it is getting a tremendous amount of attention and rapidly growing in popularity. The Enneagram considers nine different dimensions of personality. Although I'm by no means an expert on these tools, I find the Enneagram invaluable in understanding the motivation underlying human behavior. The MBTI tells you a bit more about the *hardware*, that is, how you're wired and likely to look at the world. The Enneagram looks at the reasons why you deploy your hardware the way you do.

While MBTI and Enneagram are helpful in understanding our personality types, several other tests available can be helpful on a professional front. The Highland

Ability Battery is a comprehensive assessment of particular innate abilities—that is, what are the things you are actually good at doing simply because of your wiring. Using these innate abilities, we all cultivate skills, and a tool like StrengthsFinder, for example, is a neat assessment of our primary professional skills. The Strong Interest survey can indicate areas of work we may find attractive. The Kolbe is a more recent assessment that explores in more depth how we actually go about completing our work.

Emotions

An additional component of our Self-and-Money Framework is our emotions, which undoubtedly play an important role in how we feel about the lives we're living. From a wealth perspective, it's important to acknowledge the emotional responses we're likely to have regarding our wealth. We may feel joy that we're able to engage in certain activities, or we may feel shame if we believe we're unworthy of achieving wealth the way we did. Not surprisingly, there are many counselors and psychologists who deal specifically with the emotional issues that arise from wealth.

Roles

The final core element of the framework are our roles. We all play many different roles in life. In our families, we may play the role of the responsible older child or the free-spirited ne'er-do-well. In our marriage, we may be the peacemaker. In our profession, we may be the dependable one who can always be counted on to get a project across the finish line.

Each of these roles affects how we see ourselves and is affected by and informs our interaction with wealth. If we believe that we must always be the responsible one, making financial choices that are purely for enjoyment's sake may be quite challenging.

Family, Community, and Society

The interior circle of the Self-and-Money Framework (Exhibit 6.1) focuses on wiring, emotions, self-concept, and roles as key inputs affecting our thinking about wealth. This portion of the diagram is purely internally focused, but it would be incomplete to say these four components were all we need to consider. Instead, we must recognize the two-way relationship of how these internal components interact with the broader spheres we inhabit—our families, our local communities, and the broader society (as marked in the outer squares of the diagram).

Each of those spheres has its own perceptions regarding wealth, accepted norms of behavior, and levels of interaction between those of greater or lower wealth strata. All of them play significant roles in our thinking about wealth. Let's take a closer look at each one.

Family: How our family of origin affects and shapes our daily life is one of the most underestimated factors in understanding ourselves. Although we highlighted factors related to *nature* above, the *nurturing* that occurs in our formative eighteen years at home has a sizable impact on us all. Family therapists who study family dynamics tell us that as we become autonomous individuals and establish lives of our own, how we individuate and function as members of our families is certainly one of life's challenging tasks, which we must all undertake.

And each family has its own narrative around wealth. For immigrant families, that narrative may involve the sacrifice of leaving a country of origin to seek a greater fortune elsewhere. Many families are mixed in their financial achievement, with some family members attaining significant levels of financial success while other family members remain in the same financial circumstances. Of course, there are the families who tell a more tragic tale of having once attained significant financial wealth only to see the family lose its fortune.

While each family has its own unique narrative around wealth, so does each person who "marries into" it. Differences and commonalities in narrative can mark areas of potentially explosive drama or deep alignment.

Not understanding the benefits and baggage of each of these narratives would be a major shortcoming in understanding your wealth identity

Community and Society: Understanding the structure of the society of which you're a part and where you fit within it are critical components of self-understanding. Without endorsing social class or hierarchical modes of social organization, we may still recognize the simple reality that we all find ourselves to be part of a culture that has a pecking order, whether we like it or not. Where one falls in this pecking order can result from a wide variety of factors—one's hometown, skin color, gender, vocal accent, interests, manner of speech, dress, manners. All of these various facets interact with the social environment in which you function. Of course, at the extreme, we're all familiar with the Clampetts of *The Beverly Hillbillies* television show as a truly ridiculous example of class misalignment.

Yet, more seriously, as American venture capitalist J.D. Vance so thoughtfully points out in his eloquent *Hillbilly Elegy*, there are real and meaningful differences between how different societal groups live. Personally, having grown up in a small town, I was woefully unaware there was an entirely different strata of society and style of living. Interacting regularly with that strata has required careful attention to the social mores and practices of this group.

A Step Back

There are, admittedly, a lot of moving pieces to consider in determining how the self affects your view of your wealth, but the Self and Money Framework can help you systematically walk through major elements that may be impacting your view of your wealth. Rather than going through each element individually, it may be easier to consider some high-level diagnostic questions as a more accessible on-ramp to thinking this way. These explorations would be akin to the questions your family doctor might ask during a checkup to determine the overall state of your health.

So let's begin by considering a few broader questions. I want to recognize at the outset that reading a book like this is often in response to a specific situation or set of questions you're working to answer. With those in mind, I encourage you to pull out a pad of paper and pen to jot down responses to the following questions.

- → At the current time, do you feel content with your life's circumstances?
- → Do you find your financial circumstances and practices to be a source of pride? Or frustration?
- → Do you feel shame about your wealth relative to your community of origin or your religious practice?
- → If we were to review your stated mission, vision, and values statement and compare the stated priorities to the expenses on your credit card bill, would your spending be in alignment with those priorities?
- → Do you believe that you're *good with money*? Why or why not?
- → What were some of the earliest messages you heard or thought about money?
- → How was money viewed within your family of origin?

➡ Where does work fit within your construct of wealth?

Understanding oneself is among life's most important and pressing challenges. To some extent, even answering these questions is to wrestle with that ancient question of nature versus nurture. How much of who we are is a function of our particular hard wiring and how much is due to our life's circumstances is an unanswerable question.

Understanding oneself is the great work we all must undertake over the course of our lives. Personality, motivation, interest, and skills are four common facets that provide the raw material for beginning to understand the self. Layering onto those discoveries by contemplating one's familial background, the circumstances in which you were raised, and the nature of your family of origin will shine even greater light. Finally, no man or family is an island, and understanding cultural norms and mores can offer further insight. For individuals and families of means, this cultural climate can be illuminating in shaping views of philanthropic responsibility to the broader society.

CHAPTER 7

DEFINING YOUR
WEALTH IDENTITY

"He is a great man who uses earthenware
dishes as if they were silver,
but he is equally great who uses silver as if it
were earthenware. It is the sign of an unstable
mind not to be able to endure riches."

—SENECA

———

The previous chapter was about understanding the cards you have been dealt in terms of self/emotions/ roles/wiring. We shift now to how to begin to play those cards. The natural place to begin is with what the corporate literature refers to as mission(why)/vision/values statements. At the outset, it is important to acknowledge the varying viewpoints and experience we all bring to those statements. Some of us come from strong corporate and organizational cultures where such statements are a part of a lived reality. For others, they were an exercise engaged in on a corporate retreat and landed on a bookshelf gathering dust. And yet for still others, they are a blunt instrument used at best to create culture—inauthentic—or at worst to brainwash.

But at its core, each statement serves a noble purpose. Mission statements are easy to get confused with vision statements, so I prefer to refer to them as *why* statements. They answer the question *What are we doing all this for?* Value statements accompany mission statements and talk about how we conduct ourselves. The mission statement combines with values then to inform and shape a vision, a statement of what the future could look like if we are successful in executing our mission within the constraints of our values. We will consider each statement in turn.

The Why (or Mission or Purpose) Statement

Simon Sinek did the world a great favor in his TED Talk and accompanying book, *Start with Why*. Sinek's broader point, with which I agree, is that focusing on a specific outcome makes no sense unless you know where you are going in the first place. For most companies, this *why* is outlined in a mission statement. It discusses what the organization is to be about.

Let's consider two examples:

→ Nike: To bring inspiration and innovation to every athlete in the world

→ Coca-Cola: To refresh the world; to inspire moments of optimism and happiness; to create value and make a difference

These mission statements in many ways are agnostic in terms of time and place. They clearly point to what the company is about. Nike is about supporting athletes. Coke is about refreshment and that ineffable moment when you pop open one of their beverages. Individuals and families can create a similar mission statement. Doing so helps to narrow the possibilities and provide a clear sense of focus.

The crafting of a personal mission statement requires uninterrupted time and thoughtful consideration. It requires mining more deeply into the question of why you're here and why you do the things you do. These answers may be deeply influenced and even directed by your personal faith.

Although ultimately these questions are extremely personal, a few thoughts come to mind as to how to begin answering them. First, make a list of the top five to ten moments you felt most purposeful or directed in your life, work, or recreation. After completing the list, read through each of them and thoughtfully consider what it was about the experience that attracted you to engage in it in the first place. Afterward, what did you find compelling about the experience? How has the experience changed the way you function and live your life? Have you engaged in similar experiences since then?

There are a lot of resources about mission statements on the Internet, and I do not presume to have much that would be additive to those.

The Challenge of Values

To be brutally honest, although I can easily buy into the concept of a mission statement, core-values statements always seem to me like a cop out. Generally, they devolve into such generic and broad categorical terms that they become essentially meaningless. Affirming values of hard work, responsibility, and fun are common tropes in corporate values statements, but they're about as generic as motherhood and apple pie.

Values statements are often pushed through the corporate human resources apparatus and delivered to the masses as printed vinyl signage on headquarters walls or smoothly laminated cards to be distributed en mass to the hoi polloi of the organization.

The key issue is that these terms—because of their generic structure—serve no purpose in guiding decision-making. Values statements should be thought of as a toolbox that can be deployed when decisions are being made. In my experience in organizations, every company/ culture has values, whether articulated or not, that are used when decisions are being made. They function like a sieve to separate out actions that are incongruent with the goals of the organization. To be meaningful, values statements must articulate the aims that are actually driving the organization and then be reinforced and referenced when making decisions.

For values to be meaningful, I believe they must be something for which you're willing to suffer. As you continue down the path toward fulfilling your mission statement, you will be presented with opportunities and challenges. What you say yes or no to will be bound by what you believe is important. Undoubtedly, life will present opportunities that run counter to these beliefs.

So how do you begin developing this list? I would argue that there are a few values that come to mind very quickly as nonnegotiable. Thinking through several of the significant choices you've made in life and conducting a decision-making autopsy to recreate your thought process and why you made the choices you did will be instructive as well. Consider why you chose a specific college, your spouse, your first job, the first job you quit to take another job, the first major consequence you delivered to a disobedient child. Each of those circumstances is loaded with meaning and is informed by the values you hold dear.

After creating a list of four to six of these decisions, a number meaningful enough to you to provide real direction, make a simple, pithy statement to accompany the value, further explaining the meaning of each. For example, one of my personal core values is hard work. What this means to me is *attempting to perform with excellence in all things.*

After further articulating the value, it may be helpful to consider it again and ask whether or not you would be willing to hold to it in the event it cost you a modest sum of money. Not a life or death issue, but enough pain to force you to stop and think it through. If those values are nonnegotiable, then you've likely come close to articulating your values.

Vision Statement

The task of creating a vision statement is perhaps the most difficult you'll encounter in the process of creating a blueprint for your financial wealth. There are several reasons for this. Articulating a vision seems almost foolhardy in a world undergoing such rapid change and perhaps for lives that can seemingly change on the turn of a dime. Whether good fortune or tragedy befalls us, in today's world, it seems an ultimate act of hubris to describe a detailed end state for the future.

Yet not having any sense of future direction seems just as foolhardy. This, of course, was Alice's gamble in responding to the Cheshire Cat. So is there a middle way, a Monetesque impression of the ultimate destination, perhaps, rather than something as precise as Vermeer might render? I think so, and I would argue that we follow Warren Buffett's business partner Charlie Munger's maxim: "Invert, always invert." So rather than considering what we want out of life, we perhaps consider what we want out of death.

It may seem a bit morbid to begin by contemplating one's mortality, but I would argue that since death is a certainty for all of life, it's a sensible place to begin. The topic of death, of course, brings up such common refrains as *there are no hearses with trailers*, which generally are used to advocate a lifestyle free from excessive consumption.

New York Times columnist David Brooks has highlighted the importance of the ultimate fate in his construction of the concepts of resumé virtues and eulogy virtues, as discussed in his book *The Road to Character*. Brooks's broader point can be summarized this way: the virtues we list on our resumés are often contradictory to the final remarks delivered at someone's funeral.

I was struck by this dichotomy not long ago as I attended the funeral of my beloved grandfather and then many months later attended the funeral of a friend who had passed tragically in his early thirties due to substance abuse, leaving behind a wife and two children, suddenly wrecked by the task of building a life without a father.

My grandfather lived a long, full life, passing away at the age of eighty-seven. I was given the esteemed privilege by my family of eulogizing him at his funeral services. I spent three full days writing and practicing the delivery of my remarks, so I was able to give a full consideration of the man, his life, and the legacy he left behind. The words I shared centered around the love he shared with his family, his keen curiosity for the world around him, his love of story, and the great way he enjoyed the world around him.

Never mind the fact that the man was an accomplished gynecologist who had delivered thousands of babies and cared for patents for decades. What stood out at the end were words like *love, curiosity,* and *enjoyment.* And yet with a life defined by such simple and perhaps quaint virtues, an eighty-seven-year-old man's funeral was packed with family, friends, and the family of friends whose lives had been touched by the life he lived. What a great legacy to aspire to.

So as we consider the vision for our lives, I believe we must navigate the tension of being precise enough to highlight specific things that are important to us, all the while being careful to connect those things to the pieces of ourselves that are core to our identity—and likely to be all that remains of us after our passing.

Digging into this broader question of life vision begins to meld into the domain of life planning and personal coaching, where the literature is arguably a bit sparse. There are two resources I've found very helpful in these areas. The first is strategic-planning consultant Tom Paterson's *Living the Life You Were Meant to Live.* Paterson, who had a long, successful career in the corporate world began to serve as a professional mentor later in life and ultimately founded the Paterson Institute, which works with clients in an intensive format to develop their life plans. The second resource is financial life planner George Kinder's *Life Planning for You,* which covers many of the same themes found in Paterson's work. In reading Paterson and Kinder, I've tried to synthesize an approach toward addressing a life plan. I've also included exercises from my own work that have been helpful in constructing a larger vision.

To articulate a larger life vision, I find it personally helpful to begin with some questions and exercises designed to bring to the surface how you think and feel about your life currently. So let's start with some big-picture questions.

First, consider the three questions that American business consultant and religious leader Clayton Christensen raised in his essay (and later book) *How Will You Measure Your Life?*

1. How can I be sure I'll be happy in my career?
2. How can I be sure my relationships with spouse and family become a source of happiness?
3. How can I be sure to stay out of jail?

I also like to reread Jim Collins's essay "Best New Year's Resolution? A 'Stop Doing' List." Collins highlights the two questions a mentor of his asked him, which he calls the twenty-ten assignment. First, what would you change in your life if you woke up tomorrow with $20 million (that is, no financial worries to speak of)? Second, what would you change if you had less than ten years to live?

George Kinder asks a set of questions similar to those Collins poses but adds an instructive third question: What if you found out you had one day to live? What did you miss out on in life? What would you change?

After working through those questions, which are over-arching and all encompassing, I like to dig in more deeply to where I am at the moment. I consider where I am on a spectrum with regard to ambition and drive. We are often warned about the dangers of ambition. Our pop culture alone is chock full of cautionary tales of the workaholic who loses it all. Yet ambition is not without its benefits.

The same dynamic is true with regard to being driven to achieve. The desire to pursue accomplishment and mastery is arguably among the most noble. Yet left unchecked, it can destroy both self and family. Professor of marketplace theology and leadership R. Paul Stevens highlights a tension between selfish ambition and what he terms *redeemed ambition*. Selfish ambition is marked by relentless striving and restlessness. Redeemed ambition is purposeful in its direction: "neither passively quiet, nor frantically busy."

Professor of corpus linguistics Mark Davies highlights a similar tension between being called or driven. He aptly notes, "Driven people live in a world of self-created delusion marked with grandiosity and an excessive need for control." Those who are driven are filled with anxiety.

As you consider your present state as a platform for the future, it's worthwhile to question and see if your life is filled with restlessness or purposeful direction? Is it filled with forward movement but not overwhelmed by anxiety?

As we discuss in the vision-setting process, there are four areas of life that must be contemplated, four bottom lines. They are self, family, community, and vocation. As you take stock of your life, consider for each one what is right, what is wrong, what is currently confusing, and what is missing. In crafting a personal vision statement, we must consider each of the four major constituent elements of life: self, family, vocation, and community.

Self

Crafting a vision for the self requires answering the question of who you are. Who we are (or desire to be) is often best considered in terms of who we want to be remembered as. I considered the question by further segmenting the self into the concepts of mind, body, and soul.

In exploring mind, I considered David Brooks's eulogy virtues. I developed a list of six different attributes I would like to be remembered for. Many of these virtues align nicely and, in many cases, use language very similar to my core values statements. I hope who I am and what I value most become significantly intertwined over the course of time.

For body, it's important to articulate your views of your personal health, that is, the physical reality with which you engage your world. Choosing to exercise and eat sensibly is a reflection of your view of your self, just as powerful as making no choices on health and living instead an indulgent lifestyle, which may feel good in the short run but will likely affect longevity.

Finally, in considering the soul, you explore your vision of what it means to be a good and moral person, you articulate the existence of a deity, and what is required to be in good standing with that deity. As a person of faith, I have a more specific series of thoughts around what faithful living looks like and what's required for the healthy shaping of my soul. Whatever this looks like for you, it must be made explicit for it to be ultimately meaningful.

Once you've defined the mind/body/soul constituents of health, you can shift your consideration to the things you enjoy in life. Arguably, life is meant to be lived as a balance of both meaningful work and meaningful play. To articulate a comprehensive view of things you can enjoy, it's helpful to think in terms of a Venn diagram composed of the people you enjoy being with, the places you like to spend time, the activities you like to do, and the specific possessions you enjoy owning. (I'll address consumption in greater detail in Chapter 9, "How to Spend It.")

Taking stock of each element of people/places/activities/possessions that you enjoy serves as a useful framework for determining where and how you'll spend your money. In a world drowning in a million different options, it helps to narrow the playing field. Indeed, Paterson offers a question worth deep consideration: "What aren't you giving to yourself?"

Family

A vision statement must also consider the family, that is, an articulation of your vision for who you are within the family. Each family should engage in its own mission/vision/values exercise.

As I consider my role in my own family, I want to be known as an intentional and faithful husband who still regularly pursues his wife. As a father, I want to be known to each child individually and to the children as a collective entity. This means that I set goals around spending one-on-one time together with each child, as well as with all the kids.

For the family itself, it's important for you and your spouse to consider the following questions as well:

→ *If we're serious about fulfilling our mission consistent with our values—with the money we consume—what are the key hallmarks of this lifestyle?*

For my own family unit, we believe the following to be the key points of our vision.

→ *Family time.* Our lives are busy and there are many competing demands for our time including our marriage, our kids and their activities, social engagements, nonprofit causes, and the like. We want to make sure that the time we invest in these things supports the things we enjoy doing and cultivates the people we personally want to become.

To support those efforts, we're happy to pay housekeepers, yard services, and the like. Although I spent my time cleaning our house and pushing a broom during my early jobs, the addition of three to four hours to our family time each week is a good trade for the reasonable sum we spend on a housekeeper. We've found that doing so allows us to help support a hard-working family and allows us to interact with a circle beyond our own. We hope this keeps us grounded.

➤ *Leisure activities.* How can we put money into doing things we enjoy as a family?

➤ *Travel.* Travel is extremely important to my wife and me. We're willing to make sacrifices in our budget to fund additional travel.

➤ *House.* We aspire to have a house nice enough for anyone—either Queen Elizabeth or Mother Theresa—to cross our threshold and be as comfortable. As such, we want to create a warm, welcoming environment, but we're willing to perhaps spend less on home furnishings/accessories in order to free up resources for other priorities, such as travel. We purchase things for the home, firmly using the Land's End standard (see Chapter 9, "How to Spend It"), aiming for good quality at a reasonable price. Where possible, we look to "hack" our way to nicer items by buying them used on Craigslist, or, in the case of art, buying directly from new, emerging artists on Instagram, Etsy, and other social marketplaces.

Vocation

Crafting your vision for your vocation begins with an assessment of oneself and understanding your unique talents along with your particular interests. Although the concept of *passion* is often quickly mentioned when discussing work, call me a passion skeptic. There is a nicely growing body of literature that supports the idea that passion is not an ex ante phenomenon for a large portion of the population. Although there are always a few folks who've known since the age of eight that they wanted to be a doctor, for most of us, this is not the normal experience.

Instead, as Cal Newport describes in his book *So Good They Can't Ignore You,* enjoyable work derives from cultivating a unique and valuable skill set and exercising it with a degree of autonomy alongside a compelling team with a greater vision that you're excited to be part of.

In my personal experience, thinking in terms of skill development, self-direction/autonomy, within a compelling team/vision, has proved to be a valuable north star in evaluating career opportunities, as well as exploring when it's time to make a career change. As you begin to craft a career vision for yourself, outlining goals for each of those categories would be a reasonable starting place.

Community

Of course, the self does not exist alone. We've discussed the self in light of the family and work, which—considering the allocation of one's most precious resource, *time*—are likely to be the two largest investments we make. That said, we move and exist as members of a broader community as well.

This community likely includes the other members of your religious practice, your town/city, and could even be more expansive to include an ethnic group or a region of the world. How we interact with the whole of humanity is a vital piece of our self-conception. It provides anchoring against the ups and downs of life as we place ourselves in humanity's broader story.

As I'll discuss further in the Chapter 12, "Philanthropy," our thoughts concerning community and our role in it will offer vital input in influencing how we direct our philanthropic investments.

Conclusion

Only after working through each component of self, family, work, and community, and in light of the broader questions highlighted earlier in this section, is it possible to draft a vision statement. In my experience, the first draft is likely to feel lacking—either too optimistic to feel tied to reality or not specific enough to be of much value. More likely, only after further reflection will you be able to refine your vision to the right degree.

SECTION THREE

———

WEALTH
STRATEGY

BUILDING A WEALTH STRATEGY

*"All I ask is the chance to prove that
money can't make me happy."*

—COMEDIAN SPIKE MILLIGAN

———

We now shift to taking the wealth structure we explored in Section One and marrying it to wealth identity, discussed in Section Two, to create a defined and implementable wealth strategy.

In a corporate setting, strategy-setting follows a similar path. A company takes the market structure including external factors of the business (competitive dynamics of the industry and political/environmental/social/technological conditions) and internal factors (resources/processes) and unites them with its corporate identity. It brings those two elements together in pursuit of driving the greatest possible value, generally accepted as some sort of shareholder return.

Applying the Insights of Corporate Strategy to a Personal Plan

It's a challenge to apply corporate insights in a different context. In a for-profit business, the rules of the game are clearly defined. A company functions in a marketplace where profits are to be made whenever sales proceeds exceed the costs of creation. Competitors enter the market, to the extent they are able, with differing products in an attempt to capture their slice of the profit pool. Generally, human nature being what it is, we're reticent to allow any one person or company to obtain the right to a printing press of free money by allowing them to capture the entirety of the available profits in a marketplace. In fact, when it appears that a single company is becoming too powerful and remains unchallenged (that is, when a monopoly is being established), government will often step in to promote additional industry competition.

In defining a wealth strategy, our challenge is less clear because the nature of the game is much murkier. In a business world, strategy is about how to respond to competition in order to win. The nature of the game is more or less presupposed. The question is how to function best within the rules as they have been defined.

What then is the game or purpose of life for which we're articulating a strategy? That is not necessarily a straightforward question with a simple answer. The cultural constructs within which we live play an important role in shaping our view of what the good life is. Certainly as well, one's religious practice may also offer greater insight into such questions. But to attempt to postulate a universal view, arguably the goal of any wealth strategy is to promote a person's flourishing on earth. In developing an approach toward flourish, a strategy that is fully articulated will answer questions such as what is the end point of accumulation? What is the right level of consumption? What is my relationship with risk? What is my responsibility to provide for future generations? What is my responsibility to those who have less?

Introducing the Strategy Framework

To successfully integrate wealth into our lives, we must have a concrete sense of the financial choices we're making, what our priorities are, account for any constraints/considerations, and have a feedback mechanism to measure how we're tracking relative to our strategic plan.

Strategy will describe how you implement the vision in light of the positive choices we've described and the constraints you've outlined as well. The strategy framework outlined here is also summed up and available at www.davidcwellsjr.com/book. There are four primary dimensions that your wealth strategy must address: spending, investing, giving, and legacy.

Simply put, an articulated and robust wealth strategy bridges the gap between financial resources and vision by laying out an overall strategic goal, with specific, articulated goals for spending, investing, giving, and legacy. In the coming chapters, we'll look deeply at the questions of consumption, investment, philanthropy, and legacy to help you as you work to articulate your strategic goals. We'll also outline the process of taking this large-scale strategy and making it digestible through the creation of annual goals, along with a reporting mechanism.

CHAPTER 8

HOW TO SPEND IT

"A calm and modest life brings more happiness than the pursuit of success combined with constant restlessness."

—ALBERT EINSTEIN

——

To live strategically with money begins with addressing the question of consumption head on. Consumption is a touchy subject for all of us. At the basest of levels, consumption is how we begin to satisfy the lowest levels of psychologist Abraham Maslow's hierarchy of needs. Yet the reality for most of us in the Western world is that we are so far above the base of Maslow that such a distinction is nearly meaningless.

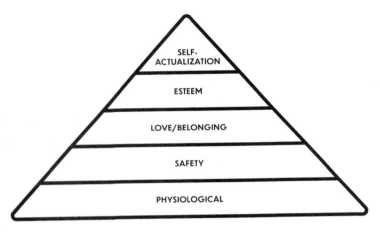

EXHIBIT 9.1 MASLOW'S HIERARCHY OF NEEDS

Source: Abraham Maslow, *A Theory of Human Motivation*

After more or less meeting basic needs, we quickly move to the more tender areas, where consumption is used to meet psychological, identity, and self-fulfillment needs. As such, as we articulate a strategy for wealth, it's important to carefully weigh such matters.

Scholars like Maslow have long attempted to answer the question of why we consume what we consume. Early twentieth century sociologist Thorstein Veblen noted, "The basis on which good repute in any highly organized industrial community ultimately rests is pecuniary strength; and the means of showing pecuniary strength, and so gaining or retaining a good name, are leisure and a conscious consumption of goods." Veblen's Theory of the Leisure Class coined the term *conspicuous consumption* and probed deeply into how goods serve our self-actualization needs.

In a mid-to-late industrial society, Veblen's theory seemed well founded. Yet over the past thirty to forty years, as we've shifted to our information age, conspicuous consumption has shifted again. *New York Times* columnist David Brooks described in his bestseller *Bobos in Paradise* how after the second world war, society began to shift its hierarchy away from pedigree toward meritocracy. People began to define themselves through accomplishments and credentials.

One only has to look at the inflation rate of higher education over this period of time versus the overall average inflation rate to see this play out. University of Southern California professor Elizabeth Currid Halkett continues Brooks's and Veblen's considerations in her book *The Sum of Small Things: A Theory of the Aspirational Class.* Halkett points out that capitalism's success has diffused conspicuous consumption so broadly it's a meaningless distinction, that is, luxury goods have become so broadly available in most categories that they no longer serve as the social signaling tools they once did. The term *accessible luxury* is emblematic of this trend. Of course, there are still some consumer brands that constitute luxury and are priced so that they require some thought before purchase even by the 0.10 percent and 0.01 percent. Think Hermes, Richard Mille, etc.

Halkett notices instead that the vast majority of the wealthy are now using other sorts of signaling to indicate status. This could be things like health and exercise trends (think Barry's Bootcamp and Soul Cycle, for example) or access to such preferential health care services as concierge medicine.

Even in light of these broader sociological trends, the reality is that for all of us, the greatest portion of our financial resources will nearly always be directed toward consumption. Even if we're "supposed" to donate 10 percent, what in the world are we supposed to be doing with the other 90 percent? Despite this reality, there are almost zero resources available to help us consume well. Instead, there is a mish-mash of articles and studies that offer opinions. Frankly, many of these opinions are written by folks whose life choices are so dramatically different from our own that they either feel Quixoteesque, in their tilting at windmills, or conversely, so absolute in their tone that the baby seems to be thrown out with the bath water.

When one encounters the stronger fringe elements of the anti-consumption world—whether they be the tiny-house community, the extreme minimalists, etc.—our reaction may be one of admiration but also disbelief that such an approach to life works for those who want their kids to go to good schools, live in nice neighborhoods, play golf, or take nice vacations, etc. This means no disrespect to those communities, because I've followed closely their writings and development for more than a decade.

Instead, I think it helpful and worthwhile to consider some of their broad messages and then carefully adapt them to your desired standard of living. Before helping you articulate a consumption policy, I want to lay out a framework for thinking about consumption and invite you to consider what the best commonsense advice and academic studies show us about the realities of consumption.

First, let me say that I'm a consumer analyst at heart. I've studied consumers and consumer companies as an advisor to large money managers and as a hedge fund manager myself. As we consider consumption, I think it's helpful to recall David Foster Wallace's classic address to Kenyon College. Wallace tells the story of two young fish swimming along who happen to meet an older fish swimming the other way. He nods at them and says, "Morning, boys, how's the water?" The two young fish swim on for a bit, and eventually one of them looks over at the other and says, "What the hell is water?"

What he highlights so acutely is that there are areas in our life where we simply are unable to obtain an objective perspective because they're so instinctively part of us that they feel as natural as breathing. Our relationship to spending is no different. The money comes in, we buy things, pay bills, and the money goes out. We rest and repeat by pay period.

As we consider consumption, it's helpful to first open our eyes and say, "This is water," or in the words of Morpheus, to take the red pill and see how deep the rabbit hole [of *The Matrix*] actually goes.

With that said, history proves to be an instructive place to begin our discussion. We find ourselves at a unique place in history as Westerners right now. It's striking to many of us to understand the tidal change that has occurred in our manner of living. The last 100 years have been massive in terms of change. Consider something as simple as life expectancy. In 1916, for the average male it was 49.6; for females, 54.3 years. Now it's 78.8 years, and one of the fastest growing demographics are those over the age of 90.

Massive technological change has supported this. In the last 100+ years, vaccinations, refrigeration, phones, cars, have tamed the vagaries and much of the uncertainties of life and unleashed an unprecedented wave of prosperity largely unseen in the history of the world. In many ways our lifestyles parallel that of the true oligarchs of turn-of-the-century America—we live as good as the Rockefellers, Carnegies, etc.

These developments have changed how we live to a great degree. For many communities, as little as three generations ago, families were still living predominately agrarian lifestyles. As the Federal Reserve Bank of St. Louis's data indicate, farm employment has shrunk from 8 million to just barely 2 million since the year 1948.

More recently, agricultural employment was accompanied by a rise in manufacturing employment through the 1940s and 1950s. Yet as the global economy grows more integrated and computing power is unleashed, manufacturing as a percentage of total jobs has fallen to record lows. And a massive increase in the level of disposable income has been unleashed.

Accompanying this massive increase in standard of living has been an accompanying effort *to spend our way to happiness.* Until 1992, the personal savings rate in the United States oscillated between the 7.5 and 10 percent range. Then, in 1992, things went into hyperdrive as the savings rate went from 9.9 percent to its low, in July 2005, of 1.9 percent. Moreover, these changes account for the massive leveraging of the consumer that occurred simultaneously. Even as the savings rate dove toward zero, households added a staggering amount of debt.

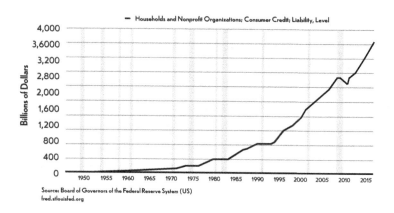

EXHIBIT 9.2 – HOUSEHOLD DEBT OUTSTANDING

The impact of this massive growth in consumption has not been pretty. From 1998 to 2012, the number of self-storage units doubled. There are now 48,500 mini warehouses in existence, with 2.3 billion square feet of space for lease and total industry revenues of $24 billion.

The UCLA Center on the Everyday Lives of Families, which has been studying the lives of American families, published a book called *Life at Home in the 21st Century*, which was a deep dive inside thirty-two homes. The researchers note, "What distinguishes us is the normative expectation of hyper-consumerism: American middle-class houses, especially in Los Angeles, are capacious; refrigerators are larger than elsewhere on the planet. Even so, we find food, toys and other purchases exceeding the confines of the home and overflowing into garages, piled up to the rafters with stockpiled extra stuff." Seventy-five percent of garages are no longer able to hold cars because they've turned into storage space.

Whether it's due to clutter or fast fashion, we've consumed at a breathtaking rate over the past thirty years or so. And yet, ironically, in the last couple years one of the books on the *New York Times* best sellers list was a little tome by a petite Japanese woman called *The Life Changing Magic of Tidying Up*.

Clutter and frenzy have not only affected our pocketbooks, balance sheets, and closets. The important question to ask is how have we as individuals and as a society responded to this sea change of activity. Theologian David F. Wells (no relation) astutely notes that "given our highly mobile society, we are not rooted in place, community, or family, and given the way that our exposure to modern life slowly empties us out, a continual sense of self has vanished for many of us. That is what makes the construction of identity necessary, whether by means of style or lifestyle."

The traditional methods of addressing the identity and self-actualization components of Maslow's hierarchy were, for most, rooted in a sense of geography, clan/tribe, and family. These were paramount in how we articulated who we were and our place in the world. Instead, we've been left bereft and tasked with the uncertain task of constructing our identity in the world. *New York Times* personal finance columnist Ron Lieber describes one way this manifests in what he terms the *dignity gauntlet*. For kids, their possessions define them rather than their peers. As such, parents feel an immense pressure to engage in *full provisioning* so as to avoid their ever having to go through the dignity gauntlet. Even the erstwhile modern poet Kanye West recognizes this existential anxiety, noting, "When we die, the money we can't keep but we prolly spend it all 'cause the pain ain't cheap'."

I would perhaps even go further and argue that the cost of excessive consumption extends beyond the individual. *Overconsumption crowds out our lives by denying us the emotional and physical space to meaningfully engage in the lives of others.* As I've studied, prayed over, and contemplated these developments, I am and have been distressed by the deep-seated divides I see in our society. In houses and lives packed full, when and how are we able to make room for the lives of others? In a society separated by differences, where and how are we? Am I letting my own privilege be not about personal entitlement and gain but about being a blessing for others?

Please note, I am not anti-consumption; instead, recall our efforts to see *"the water"* as David Foster Wallace encouraged. The great challenge of culture is that we are simply unable to get the perspective necessary to determine what is universal and normative and what is local and specific. What I'm pushing back against are the default settings of modern society that manipulate us into assuming that a life and pattern of consumption is not just desired, but normal.

Consuming Well

In *A Slip of the Keyboard,* English author Terry Pratchett writes:

> "If you're vertically wealthy, you think, *I am rich. So I had better do what rich people do.* What do rich people do? Well, they find out where the hell Gstaad is, and then they go skiing there. They buy a yacht. They may go to beaches a long way away. Well, first of all, never buy a yacht. Yachts are like tearing up hundred-pound notes while standing under a cold shower. But horizontal wealth means not letting your increased income dictate your tastes. You like books and now you have money? Buy more books! Change those catenary bookshelves for good hardwood ones! In my case, build a library extension to your office. And, of course, you buy what will be useful for that most wonderful

of pursuits, blind research, which is research without direction for the sheer joy of it."

As we consider our own consumption, it's helpful to reflect on both timeless wisdom as well as what psychological research indicates as wisely directive of consumption. Beneficial consumption arguably begins with answering some key questions: What are our deepest dreams? What do we really want out of life? What is clearly not working? Is it defining ourselves by whatever Madison Ave. has served up as the next thing? We should be on-guard against immediately jumping to the conclusion that something commercially available can answer these deepest of questions.

Deep down, we want easy answers, life hacks to the questions of how much to spend and where. Yet wisdom with regard to consumption involves much more. It requires balancing a sense of paradox. How will we know we're balancing well? We'll see and feel things that look like contentment in our lives. We're able to enjoy what we have but also be generous to those who have less. Pastor Scott Sauls of Nashville noted that this often tangibly manifests if we live toward the lower end of our income bracket. Are we consuming for the purposes of enjoyment or identity?

Of course, Christian religious teaching has been correct for centuries in warning against the dangers of envy and covetousness. Charlie Munger, Warren Buffett's curmudgeonly business partner, is quick to note that envy is the only deadly sin that is not any fun.

Defining Our Financial Goals and Marking the End Point of Our Consumption

The book *Your Money or Your Life*, by Vicki Robin, Joe Dominquez, and Mr. Money Mustache, does an excellent job in explaining that the benefits of consumption follow an inverted *U* curve. There is a point where an additional level of consumption will not, in fact, bring more happiness but may lower your overall happiness.

I would argue that having a clear end point for consumption is a helpful indicator that tells us where our point of *enough* is. Alan Barnhart, of Barnhart Crane in Memphis, is an excellent example of this, having defined early on where his consumption end point is and then using proceeds above that to fund larger priorities such as giving to charity.

But this is not an argument against consumption. In fact, I would argue that there can be great joy derived from physical goods. As we discussed in Chapter 4, "Psychology: Money's War on Our Brains," it's important to understand what's going on in our brains when we consume. That way we can determine when we consume what is in fact bringing happiness or joy and what is serving other means, such as combating insecurity, etc. This end point is unique to each of us and is heavily influenced by the era and place in the world in which we find ourselves. As has been well documented, how we feel about our wealth is significantly influenced by those around us.

So what are some guideposts we can use as we consider our consumption?

How Necessary Is Budgeting?

Consuming well does not necessarily mean you need a budget. Someone may need to help financial advisor Dave Ramsey off the floor. Here is the challenge with budgets: 99 percent of people don't do them because they're simply a pain to do. I held off 1 percent because there are people (this author included) who love budgets, spreadsheets, data, and tracking to such an extent that they would do them no matter what level of net worth they had, even if there was no way that they could possibly run out of money.

The vast majority of wealthy individuals and clients I've interacted with have an instinctual understanding of how much they're spending, but likely not a precise dollar figure. For those folks, setting boundaries on consumption through the use of automating savings programs, etc., is frankly a much easier and better use of time than knowing to the second decimal place how much they spent eating out last month.

A caveat to that: If you're in a financial position where your checking account is consistently running low each month, you're running sizable credit card bills, your closets and house are stuffed full with purchases, then a budget would likely be a helpful interim tool to change your consumption habits.

Appropriately Valuing Your Time

A primary input to thoughtful consumption is a keen understanding of the value of your time. For some, this can be calculated easily by taking your annual salary and dividing by an estimated number of hours worked to get a true hourly rate. Others, who work in terms of billable hours, have a keen sense of the value of their time.

This matters because many of us agonize so much over small trivial purchases or spend so much time overshopping for an item that we're actually worse off when we account for the time we spent reaching a decision. Spending an extra $50 in time and gas money to drive thirty minutes to pick up something that you found for $20 less makes absolutely zero sense.

This does not necessarily mean purchasing things in a profligate manner—as we'll discuss in greater detail—but rather that we should do a true accounting of the cost of an item, which includes the time required to reach a decision, rather than focusing only on the price that appears on the American Express bill.

So let's shift now to how we should spend our money.

Recognizing the Phenomenon of Declining Margin Utility

Over the past several years, a concept known as the $75,000 rule has gotten a decent amount of publicity. Researchers at Princeton note that up to the $75,000 level, happiness and money are correlated.[5] Each additional dollar of income is accompanied by a commensurate degree of happiness. Yet as one's income approaches and breaches through that $75,000 level, the relationship begins to tail off.

I would caution that the study data is a few years old, so we should adjust the $75,000 level for inflation as well as taking into consideration where someone lives and the relative cost of living. Yet despite those adjustments, the message is the same, there is not some pot of gold of additional happiness the wealthy have access to. At some point, the wealth does not move the needle as much as other items.

I think we know instinctively this is true. In my experience, I've seen highly compensated individuals, operating under a sales-quota driven pay model, who reach a very nice standard of living and have very little desire to work the additional time required to drive their income to higher levels.

Semler's Rule—the Bounds of Practicality

Ricardo Semler, South American businessman and author of the books *Maverick* and *The Seven Day Weekend,* discusses in the latter what he calls his "$15 million rule". Semler's basic point is that at a certain level of net worth, you're able to have the lifestyle benefits of being upper income, but anything beyond that point tips into inefficiency.

5 http://content.time.com/time/magazine/article/0,9171,2019628,00.html

Take, for example, Exhibit 9.3, prepared by UCLA researchers.

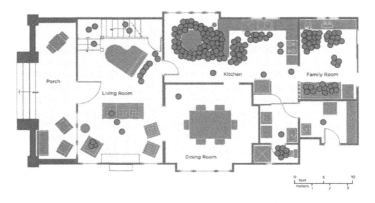

EXHIBIT 9.3

The researchers looked at where individuals spent the majority of their time in a house. The results are somewhat unsurprising given how we all tend to live our lives. Families spend their time in three primary places, the kitchen/casual dining space, the small den, and the bedroom. The makes sense because we're communal creatures who enjoy sharing meals. A small den is cozy and feels homier compared to a large, formal living space, and then we have to sleep somewhere.

As such, regardless of the ultimate size of the house, human behavior does not change to reflect the increase in square footage. In *Richistan*, by Robert Frank, one retired multimillionaire notes about his palatial Upper East Side home, "It's not comfortable. Sometimes you don't know until you're living in a space, but this feels too big for two people. There are no cozy areas."

This is by no means a polemic against large homes. Many people who have large homes use them to a great extent for regular entertaining, etc. Instead, it's more a caution that you should thoughtfully consider the size of the home relative to your needs (and in light of your other priorities).

It can be helpful to do so by considering the cost per room and cost per use of additional infrequently used square footage. For example, in the house I grew up in, we had both a formal family living room and dining room, which were used around the major holidays Thanksgiving, Christmas, and Easter. So take the estimated square footage of your unused space and multiply by the going cost per square foot of real estate in your area. So in Nashville, where I'm based, assume a formal dining room of 400 square feet at $250 per foot has $100,000 of value. Assuming a standard 20 percent down payment and a 5 percent mortgage, you're spending a little over $5,000 a year for the privilege of having that space. If that room is used three times a year, the cost per use is about $1,600.

Place that figure against the cost of a private dining room at a restaurant with a $1,000 minimum, and consider that at least at the restaurant you don't have to do the dishes when the meal is done.

Money Worth Spending

The research is pretty clear that there are some things that are meaningful in driving an increase in absolute happiness. The nonprofit 80,000 Hours, which works to improve workforce engagement, has a tremendous database at https://80000hours.org/articles/money-and-happiness/, which looks explicitly at where and how money is related to happiness. Here are a few of the summary conclusions:

First, get healthy. Improving the quality of one's health can be equivalent to the increase in happiness derived from a 6,351 percent increase in your income level.

Second, improve the quality of your marriage. Improving the happiness of one's marriage can be equivalent to seeing a 767 percent increase in your income (as noted by Ball & Chernova).

Third, pick experiences over ownership. There is good research data that supports the view that experiences provide greater enjoyment than ownership of possessions.

But that's not a panacea either. Although the data indicates that experiences are more positive toward happiness, the anticipation is more enjoyable than the ultimate outcome. We can only enjoy the process if we are not too attached to the eventual conclusion.

How to Buy

First, it's helpful to recognize that the biggest elements of consumption in our lives are shaped heavily by our stage of life. Harry Dent in his book *The Demographic Cliff* (which skews a bit hyperbolic about the challenges that face modern economies) is helpful in noting the life cycle of consumption and the typical categories in which consumers spend as they age. This is helpful in assuming that your consumption desire or need is somehow unique to you and your circumstances. In many cases, it's highly informed by your stage of life and what accompanies that stage (see Exhibit 9.4).

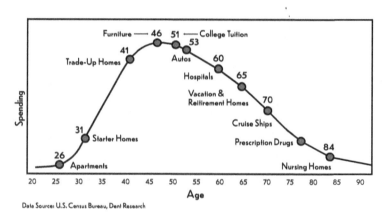

Data Source: U.S. Census Bureau, Dent Research

EXHIBIT 9.4

The Lands' End Rule for Consumption

New York Times columnist Ron Leiber refers to the Lands' End rule in their household. When a child wants some sort of an item, he and his wife are willing to provide a Lands' End level of quality, that is, a nice, middle-level quality item that should last a reasonable length of time.

Of course, even finding such middle-quality items has become more and more challenging. As Michael Silverstein and Neil Fiske note in their book *Trading Up,* consumer goods are increasingly becoming bar-belled in their price/quality. At one end, you have things that are house brands and often low quality, whether they're from a mass-market retailer like Target or a fast-fashion purveyor like a H&M or Zara. Conversely, the successful brands of the modern era have taken each product category to an almost excessive level of quality or craftsmanship, stopping at two price points—the accessible-luxury price point and the full-luxury price point. Accessible luxury is represented by Michael Kors and Tory Burch at the low/mid-end to Gucci/Louis Vuitton on the higher end. At the true luxury end, you have flagship brands like Hermes and Patek Phillipe.

As such, it's important to recognize the classic categories of need versus want. But even within those areas, consider cost per use and other factors that may sway you toward buying something more expensive. *Less but better* is a phrase heard often as consumers look to own less items but of better quality, which should last many years. For many luxury items, it's even becoming possible to rent luxury and buy utility. Recognizing the limited number of uses (and accompanying high cost per use), many new companies have arisen to provide access to luxury goods at an in between price point. Examples such as VRBO and Airbnb provide both low-end and luxury properties available to rent. Or consider Rent the Runway, which offers access to designer dresses and apparel for less cost per wear.

Fixed- Versus Variable-Cost Structure

We've all heard the horror story of someone in the community who's forced by choice or circumstance to materially alter their standard of living downward. Perhaps the most wonderful example of this is the tremendous documentary by Lauren Greenfield called *The Queen of Versailles*. Released in 2012, the film follows Jackie and David Siegel, owners of a large time-share company, as they undertake the construction of one of the most expensive private residences in the United States. Like all such projects that begin near the peak of an economic cycle, the construction is affected dramatically by the global financial crisis and ultimately comes to a halt. The family is forced to lay off household staff etc.

In management accounting, it's helpful to distinguish between fixed and variable for understanding contributions to profit margins. In much the same vein, it's valuable for households to consider the same types of categorizations when they put together a budget. Things like the mortgage payment look a lot like fixed expenditures. Although they can be changed, doing so is time consuming and expensive (for example, 6 percent real estate commission). Compare that to lawn-care service. Lawn-care service is a helpful practical luxury for large numbers of people, but if worse came to worse, it could be set aside without too much fuss.

Why this matters is the simple reality of how miserable a downward adjustment to standard of living is combined with the heightened degree of economic uncertainty we all sense in a world whose rate of change is increasing at what feels like an exponential pace. For those who generate their wealth by income/savings, having an understanding of the levers that can be pulled when cash flow moves around is of vital importance.

Of course, I have yet to meet anyone at any level of net worth who is not affected by movements in the markets. Even the most well-heeled likely made some lifestyle adjustments during the global financial crisis, so regardless of net worth, having a sense of the moving components of your consumption and how they can be adjusted up or down is only prudent.

Truly Discretionary Spending

"To arrive at a similarly peaceful mindset without riding the whole shopping roller coaster," Manisha Thakor, a financial advisor, recommends a different approach entirely, one that's known within life-coaching circles as the *be, do, have* paradigm shift. "What I've noticed is this: The people who aren't ruled by their stuff start the day thinking, 'This is the kind of person I want to *be*,'" Thakor notes. "They are rooted in the question of who and how they want to be in this world. That enables them to *do* certain things, which enables them to *have* certain stuff, but they aren't attached to those things, because their primary identity is already fulfilled."[6]

Lest you feel this message is being taken too far, removing all fun from consumption, let me remove all doubt. Enjoying things in our lives is one of life's true pleasures. The chance to own something produced by a true craftsman brings great pleasure during each use and can be treasured for many lifetimes.

Yet in a modern Western culture, our discussion to this point of caution and careful dissection of one's spending seems perhaps more appropriate, given the statistical realities of how we consume. We all have certain types of consumption that we're able to do almost without thinking, even if the consumption is beyond a budget.

Consumption, Privacy, and the Public

In today's highly connected, networked environment, it's important that each person consciously consider how public they're willing to be. Whether through social networks (where it has been said that if something is free to you, it's because *you* are the product) or the ongoing digitalization of record keeping, it's important to understand where and how you may or may not be revealing yourself to the broader public.

6 From https://www.thecut.com/2017/07/money-mom-i-feel-guilty-about-how-much-money-i-make.html

Let's conduct a hypothetical privacy audit—a type of analysis we conduct for our clients to give them a look at what may or may not be publicly viewable. The scenario is as follows: Your family takes its private jet to Turks for a long, Labor Day weekend celebration. Before leaving the fixed-based operator (FBO) private terminal, your teenage kids take a quick selfie in front of the plane, which they post to the Instagram page #bestvacationever. In the picture, the tail number of the plane is visible.

Through the tail number and a quick search of the FAA's plane registry, we find that the plane is owned by Old Mitt Aviation, LLC, a reference to your glory years playing college baseball. Interesting, our resourceful investigative journalist notes, and pulls up the Department of State's website for the state of incorporation and searches for the annual report filing that all companies are required to make to their state of registration. In that filing, a mailing address is listed and perhaps an attorney name.

Next, he searches the database for all companies with *Old Mitt* in the name. I've found that families with internal family names or references always have more than one legal entity using that reference. Quickly, three other companies are located. Quick Google searches for those company names reveal that one of those entities is a property tax holder of record for 123 Mansion Drive in the nice part of town—pretty good odds this is the family's primary residence.

On and on down the rabbit hole it goes. Each of the entities use the same mailing address, so a quick search of that address also reveals a few other corporate entities using the same address, but located out of state. One looks as if it holds the family's vacation place in Vail—and in case there was any doubt, the same lawyer who signed the Secretary of State filing in Colorado signed for the entities in the home state. Coincidence? Likely not.

Searching for just a couple of hours, it's easy to locate the majority of the family's real estate holdings, their business assets, charitable priorities (easy pickings if they serve on board and/or make donations with their name attached), charitable tax filings (via Form 990 if they have a private foundation), private plane, and more. All of this freely available online, without hiring a private investigator.

The point of this hypothetical exercise is that it can be helpful to see how much information you're revealing about yourself online and to determine if that is something you're comfortable with. In a world where it may be easy to determine your paycheck (if you're senior management in a public company) or likely assets (in the case of a business M&A transaction, with disclosed financial figures), this level of disclosure may bring you a certain amount of attention that is of interest or not. Sadly at worst, it may invite some unplanned security considerations.

Conclusion

For substantially all people, our consumption will be the greatest single use of cash flow. Our choice of house, large-ticket consumer durables, like cars, planes, and boats, where we vacation are all complex choices that sit at the intersection of what our resources permit, what we find enjoyable, what is normal in our social circle, and what signaling we want to make to our peers about our level of success.

Each of those spheres and considerations is worth a degree of thoughtful analysis as one's wealth grows. Certainly, there is a degree of materiality to this, that is, don't agonize when you need to purchase a new serving spoon at Target. But for life's larger purchases, it seems worthwhile to begin to articulate a view on one's consumption.

By understanding yourself, your needs, and wants, you're able to consume in such a manner that you can fully enjoy what you have. By doing so thoughtfully, you limit waste and inefficiency in your spending. This efficiency becomes a marvelous resource for enabling your engagement with the three remaining strategic spheres of wealth—investing, philanthropy, and legacy.

Questions to Consider

→ When someone leaves your house following a dinner party, what do they remark about you and your home? Are you comfortable with those comments?

→ Does your standard of living prevent people from knowing the real you?

→ Does your standard of living prevent you from knowing the real you?

→ Is it true that your lifestyle should stair step with your income?

→ Is your social media use robbing you of contentment?

→ Where does enjoyment become indulgence in your life?

→ What do we do about inequality of station?

→ Where is the line between appreciation of beauty versus indulgence?

CHAPTER 9

HOW TO INVEST

"Here's the paradox: The odds are overwhelming I will end up richer by aiming for a good return rather than a brilliant return—and sleep better en route. Folks who seek a killing usually get killed... Consistency is the key. It is close to impossible to get a good, long-term rate of return if you suffer serious negative numbers en route. It's the math. A single year that is down 30 percent means you have to get 30 percent per year positive returns for the next four years to get back on track for a 15 percent annual average. Or, if you score 20 percent annually for four years, and then suffer a 30 percent decline, your five-year average return is only 7 percent."

—KEN FISHER, FORBES, 1989

———

rticulating and ultimately achieving any wealth strategy will include the development and implementation of a sensible investment program. My purpose in this chapter is not to present a comprehensive framework to generate investment success, such as identifying and selecting talented investment managers or selecting individual stocks or doing your own deals as a private investor or angel investor.

The purpose of this discussion is to frame high level thinking about the pathway to reaching longer-term investment success. We will consider such components as risk and reward, how the market works, what an articulated investment philosophy looks like, and how one builds a portfolio of investments. I'll also include a few warnings and conclude with thoughts about how to wisely select an advisor to assist with the investment process. The approach is intended to be from a high enough level that a well-educated individual could read this and follow along, without requiring advanced training in finance or mathematics.

As I've mentioned, I come from several generations of doctors, but I always had a deep interest in business. Whether it was collecting advertising brochures to store in a briefcase at the age of five, or starting my first company at seventeen, my interest in business has been long running.

Midway through my time in college, I became seriously interested in the manner in which wealth is accumulated in the business world. It was the early 2000s and the most popular books on the subject at the time were related to getting rich through the acquisition of levered real estate assets—a sign of the times.

I kept reading and in late 2004, I found a great book called *The Making of an American Capitalist,* a biography of Warren Buffett. With Buffett, I felt I was being shown for the first time an underlying process, or framework for thinking, rather than a specific technique for building wealth. Just a couple years later, I was able to meet Warren, along with a group of students from my alma mater. I also attend the annual meeting in Omaha for a number of years. This learning and interaction lit a spark that began a more than fifteen-year inquiry into the nature of the financial markets. Professionally, that has manifested itself in a few different roles. I say that at the outset to frame the discussion that follows.

Investing Begins with Understanding Risk

As we consider investing, I want to articulate a systematic and strategic way for thinking about the activity. Let's consider first at the highest of level what investing is. Investment is the act of exchanging a monetary unit today in the expectation of the return of that the unit at a later date plus a return to compensate for the risk of delay. When we make investments, we're deferring the use of those funds today in exchange for the ability to do more of that at a later date. As such, when we evaluate investments, we're generally focused on the *value exchange* that occurs.

Investing is first about the return of capital and then about the return on capital. Losing money is awful. There is no worse feeling on earth. Intuitively this makes sense because we already deferred gratification in exchange for something better tomorrow when we chose to invest. When money is lost, we lose on all forms of gratification— both today and tomorrow.

The only sensible place to begin any investment program is by contemplating what loss you're willing to tolerate. By giving up our *something extra* today, what we receive tomorrow is directly related to how long it is before the money returns and how risky it is. For something with little risk, it may be a loan to the government in the form of a Treasury bill, or it could be a loan to a company, which is secured by a building. That collateral allows the loan to be repaid through the seizure and sale of the building in the event the company defaults on the loan.

Therefore, all investors should have a keen sense of what security means to them, when they need the money back, and how much risk they're comfortable taking in the interim period. Risk, much like Supreme Court Justice Potter Stewart's warning about obscenity, is something we know when we see it. It can be very difficult to precisely articulate exactly what it means.

Arguably, absolute downside risk is paramount. I've yet to meet an investor who was actively searching for ways to lose money. Understanding exactly how much one could lose allows you to calibrate the size of your investment relative to the gain you stand to make. Knowing that risk is, at its core, about the odds of losing money; how to measure it remains a great challenge. For years, academics have used volatility as a key input for thinking about how to value an asset. Many investors, such as Warren Buffett, have argued that risk is not volatility—*it is the chance of permanent loss of capital.*

So who is ultimately correct? I think both points of view are simultaneously right and wrong—a classic paradox. Warren Buffett's mentor, Ben Graham, who taught for years at Columbia Business School, termed the nature of markets to have volatility as a character he called Mr. Market. On any given day, Mr. Market will offer to buy or sell your stocks. You just have to keep in mind that he is schizophrenic.

There are days when investments get marked to cheap prices and days when they get valued richly. The investor's job is to keep a calm head and try and ascertain a reasonable estimate of what a sensible buyer would be willing to pay for a given asset. Although there may be bumps in the road, in general over a two-to-three-year period, markets figure out what the correct price is to pay for various assets. Because of the inherent uncertainty in determining the value of something, combined with the fact that human beings (for now) are subject to various emotional swings, just because the price of something fluctuates does not necessarily reflect the risk of the asset is any more or less great.

And, in fact, as value investors have demonstrated over time, when you buy something for a bargain, a lot less has to go right for an investor to have a chance at making a big return. So in that instance, the absolute risk of a permanent loss, either through a bankruptcy in the worst case or even a structural change in the business, perhaps due to competitive obsolescence is modestly lower because you bought sensibly and limited the downside risk you were exposed to. So at a micro level, this view of risk makes a great deal of intuitive sense. That's important to note.

At a macro level, however, things arguably appear a bit different. Because humans are the actual participants in the economy, we see long-term cycles of greed and fear in the markets. These long-term cycles of greed and fear, or booms and busts, lead to massive swings in the value of assets.

For a large portion of investors, the experience of those swings is structurally different. Because the composition of stock markets has changed from an environment where individual investors are the dominant holders of stocks to one where institutions are, individuals experience the swings and act differently. Rather than own companies outright, investors have outsourced those decisions directly to mutual funds that own the companies or to something as simple as an index fund. With so-called passive investments like index funds and exchange-traded funds (ETFs), the actual securities owned by an investor are just the output of a mathematical formula.

As such, when investors come into or out of markets, they generally do so as a result of greed or fear, or in an almost programmatic fashion, through retirement savings where they invest a little each month. They're not focused on the absolute downside risk of a specific investment.

They're not evaluating a company, like Home Depot for instance, and saying they think the company will continue to grow, and if this quarter was not as good, they're willing to give the company a chance. Instead, the decision is risk-on, risk-off.

Obviously, this is a simplification to some degree, but it's not as far off as you would think. As such, the question is more one of behavior than downside risk. At some point, as the market oscillates higher or lower, would the investor be unable to stay at the table or be forced to fold her hand. For many investors, that's all that matters. There is a maximum percentage or even a specific dollar amount of loss that they're willing to stomach. For someone who grew up without two nickels to rub together and put together a multi-million-dollar investment portfolio through hard work or luck, the idea of losing $2 million is unthinkable in an absolute dollar sense, even though on a percentage basis the amount may not be that significant. Emotions are what change risk from being just the downside of an investment, so that volatility management becomes of paramount importance.

Defining Your Investment Philosophy

Once you've considered carefully your views on risk, the next step in implementing an investment program is to articulate an investment philosophy. An investment philosophy is a statement of your views on the nature of financial markets and the methods by which they can be successfully navigated.

Many investment philosophies are well known and referenced regularly in the press. For example, the passive-only investment philosophy believes that markets are generally so efficient price-wise that it's a fool's errand to try to actively manage portfolios. We'd expect an investment portfolio following such a strategy to be heavy with index funds and ETFs. Value investing is another well-known philosophy. Value investors focus on buying assets that are trading at a discount for some reason. They are generally less concerned with the growth potential and instead focus on how the asset returns to a fair value from "cheap."

So let's consider a few of the various dynamics of the public markets. In the spirit of starting with the end in mind, it's helpful to remember that there are easier ways to get rich than the public markets. By my own estimate, if we look at the *Forbes* 400, 8 percent of the list derived their wealth from hedge funds and 5 percent from asset management (that is, mutual funds). As for expanding to all financial services, including private equity and venture capital, only 21 percent of the *Forbes* 400 got there through those pathways.

The great thing about the public markets is there are zero barriers to entry, but given the total number of market participants, it speaks to the difficulty. I say this as a simple warning; the vast majority of investors would be better off not participating actively in the public markets or trying to beat the market. Said differently, beating the market is a zero sum game in aggregate—you should act accordingly.

If we look at the *Forbes* 100 (the top 100 members of the *Forbes* 400 list), I estimate that 70+ percent of them were growth entrepreneurs or business owners, that is, they took existing businesses and grew them and/or bought businesses over time to make their wealth. Only 15 percent were the Henry Fords or Steve Jobs of the world, who peered further into the future than the rest of us and invented whole new products and industries. The vast majority were followers who built great businesses in existing markets. Conclusion: there are huge opportunities to grow your wealth by building a business in an existing industry and/or taking over and running an existing business better.

Let's assume that your investments in the markets are for the purpose of growing an existing asset base, not necessarily generating one, that is, we're not focusing on how to get rich in the stock market. Nevertheless, there are two fundamental questions you must settle for yourself. *First, is the market efficient or not? Second, if you're going to try to beat the market, what steps will you take to outperform?* How you answer these questions will determine how you structure your investment process.

Is the Market Efficient or Not?

What do we mean by market efficiency? In the 1960s, economists at the University of Chicago articulated a hypothesis (the efficient-market hypothesis (EMH) that investors are rational and that the stock markets are efficient—meaning that the current price for a given stock reflects all available information and, as a result, *no investor in the markets will consistently be able to achieve above-average returns,* regardless of their investment strategy, over a lengthy period of time. Obviously, in any given year, 50 percent of managers will have above-average performance and 50 percent will be below average.

For most of the investment industry, EMH has largely been adopted as fact. Practitioners of this view structure portfolios by looking at a wide range of asset classes, analyzing their historical returns and volatility, quantifying the correlation of each asset class to another, and then mathematically seeking to optimize a portfolio through a mean-variance optimization (MVO). MVO designs a portfolio that tries to create the largest possible return by blending the right amount of assets, given historical volatility and correlation for an investor's desired level of risk (using volatility as a proxy for risk).

My view is that *while markets are efficient* most *of the time, there are areas and times when they become inefficient.* I disagree with EMH proponents in describing risk as volatility. And, at the risk of being overly technical, I'm highly skeptical that modeling volatility by assuming a normal statistical distribution (a bell curve) even begins to approximate the reality of how risk behaves in the capital markets. As humans, *market participants are not always ratio-*

WHEN ANYTHING IS POSSIBLE

nal. They're prone to spells of greed (2000, 2007) and fear (1929, 2008) that cannot be explained by EMH.

As we saw in the Global Financial Crisis of 2008, when volatility increased, all assets became highly correlated (investors sold all stocks and bonds simultaneously, without differentiating between high quality and low quality). Driving permanent loss of capital was the nature of the investment opportunity, capital structure, and initial valuation paid, so if you paid too much for a share of an over-leveraged mortgage lender, you lost money, whereas if the price of your Berkshire Hathaway shares fell 50 percent, then regained their prior level, you merely experienced volatility. In my view, investment risk is similar to the underwriting analysis that a bank does when determining whom to give a mortgage to. In that scenario, the banker would define risk as the potential loss of initial capital given the credit quality of the borrower (that is, will the bank get its principal back, let alone the appropriate interest rate for the risk incurred?).

Finally, there is substantial research to support the understanding that there *are* inefficiencies in the marketplace that certain investors can take advantage of to achieve above-average returns consistently. (See the article by Warren Buffet "The Superinvestors of Graham-and-Doddsville.")

What Is Your Strategy to Outperform the Markets?

After deciding if markets are efficient or not, you have to answer the question *Where do profit-making opportunities lie?* or *Where is Bobby Fisher not playing chess?* There are generally two basic strategies that can outperform the markets consistently.

The first is value investing—buying stocks that are unloved or cheap; the second is momentum investing—buying what has been performing well most recently. Notice that we did not highlight *growth*. Although many growth stocks have high momentum, in a momentum strategy the important approach is to invest in names whose price movement has recently been favorable. These are the only two strategies where the sources of these opportunities are persistent over time (and have been documented extensively in academia).

Both of these strategies generally have an innate sense of appeal to investors. Momentum investors love the story of companies on the rise and have a keen sense of what the market is pricing in, and they have a ready finger on the trigger to add to or exit a position if they sense the story is changing for the better or worse. Value investors instinctively love the idea of "buying a dollar for fifty cents."

Building the Philosophy

With a keen understanding of risk, a view of market efficiency, and a sense of your wiring as a momentum or value investor, you can begin to build you investment philosophy. I would distinguish this philosophy from a traditional *investment policy statement* (IPS). An IPS is often constructed to aid in building the actual asset allocation, and it considers things like return criteria, tax issues, liquidity needs, etc. It forms the goal and sidelines of the actual management of the portfolio.

The investment philosophy is a statement of belief that's married with the IPS to build the allocation. It determines how the game will be played. It will often determine what opportunities should be included as possible allocations. An investment philosophy does not have to be lengthy or overly complex. Instead, a clear and concise document would follow something like the following outline.

1. What is your view on risk?
2. What game are you going to play? Track the market? Outperform?
3. Value or momentum?

Approach and Implementation

As former Secretary of Treasury Robert Rubin tells us, "Individual decisions can be badly thought through and yet be successful, or exceedingly well thought through but be unsuccessful, because the recognized possibility of failure in fact occurs. But over time, more thoughtful decision-making will lead to better overall results, and more thoughtful decision-making can be encouraged by evaluating decisions on how well they were made rather than on outcome."

Once you have articulated an investment philosophy, you can begin to think through the process by which the philosophy is implemented. In the long run, investment decision-making is a field in which the strength of the investor's process and how they make investment decisions ultimately drive success or failure. Here are the key process elements to consider:

Protect the principal. As we have covered, investors position themselves best for long-term success by focusing first on protecting the downside and then looking for upside potential. By doing so, investors get to experience the wonderful benefits of compound interest, instead of playing catch up to recover from losses. Over time, this leads to substantive differences in wealth creation.

The default investment is cash. In light of protecting the principal, I would rather hold cash and see moderate underperformance than risk capital impairment. Although some investors may park excess funds in an index fund, money market, or other instrument to earn a little yield, these parking lots are never as safe or as liquid as they seem or as promised. In the event of a market pullback, cash is a natural hedge and gives you the flexibility to move rapidly and take advantage of opportunities.

With an articulated view on how you believe the market works and a keen sense of risk appetite, you can begin to construct an asset allocation. An asset allocation is a combination of both art and science. Yet the bottom line take-away is that when a group of assets are combined in a portfolio, and those assets show varying degrees of correlation with one another, the overall portfolio shows greater upside potential with lower volatility. This ability to blend assets with various correlations highlights what has been called the only free lunch in investing—diversification. Portfolios that are sub-optimally diversified give up the potential risk/return benefits that could be obtained with essentially no incremental costs, only by changing the mix of assets.

It's helpful to think first of blending *risk-on* assets and *risk-off* assets. Risk-on assets are composed of a wide range of asset classes—equities, real assets, private equity, etc.— that are used in a portfolio for the purpose of bearing risk to generate a return. Risk-off assets are used to dampen volatility in the portfolio—ideally, they would have an inverse correlation to *risk-on* assets. Historically, bonds were the classic example of a volatility dampener. The duration of bonds and guaranteed coupon payments provide a nice offset to the volatility and uncertain payout of stocks. Interestingly, for most of recent market history, a 60/40 portfolio of stocks and bonds got 80 percent of the stock market's return, with only two-thirds the volatility—a major win for investors.

With an understanding of downside volatility and risk, you can begin to look at various scenarios for various mixes of assets and potential drawdowns you may experience in the portfolio during your investment time horizon. From that, you can begin to choose an overall risk mix that makes sense. Of course, that choice is not done in isolation, so you have to counterbalance the risk born with the likelihood of accomplishing your financial goals. Once that overall mix is set, you can begin the process of choosing the investments that fill the buckets.

Portfolio Management

Economist Benjamin Graham said, "You are neither right nor wrong because the crowd disagrees with you. You are right because your data and reasoning are right."

Once you have a portfolio in place, there are a few dynamics that are important to highlight. I would be willing to hazard a guess that the vast majority of investment literature is focused on two primary topics: finding investment ideas and investment analysis.

Here, I want to highlight a critical part of the investment process that receives very little investor attention: the actual process of making the go/no-go investment decision. This critical step is often taken for granted: once an investor identifies and analyzes a potential investment, the choice to put it into their portfolio is more or less a given.

But let me interject a note of caution and say *not so fast*. In the course of building and refining my investment approach, I've spent a considerable amount of time reading and researching human decision-making. The overwhelming finding from this reading is that while we all believe we're great at making decisions, in actuality, we're quite poor at it. I call this the Lake Wobegon effect. Lake Wobegon, from Garrison Keillor's *A Prairie Home Companion,* is "where all the women are strong, all the men are good looking, and all the children are above average."

Nobel Prize-winning psychologist Daniel Kahneman notes in his book *Thinking Fast and Slow* that heuristics, the rules of thumb we use in making decisions, are "quite useful, but sometimes lead to severe and systematic errors." Kahneman goes on to postulate that the brain functions with System 1 and System 2 thinking. System 1 is our fast thinking, or the thinking that we do using expert levels of information we may possess in our domain of expertise and any relative heuristics we can apply. System 2 thinking is the slow, deliberate process that engages the full measure of one's cognitive abilities.

There are three primary pitfalls I believe investors face: maintaining objectivity, managing complexity, and avoiding error. Each of these pitfalls arises when System 1 thinking takes over and keeps us from fully evaluating the best possible decision. Next we address each pitfall, and what I believe to be the appropriate way to engage System 2 thinking (that is, how to use your full cognitive abilities to make the best possible investment decision).

Maintaining Objectivity—Premortems

John Kenneth Galbraith pointed out, "Faced with a choice between changing one's mind and proving there is no need to do so, almost everyone gets busy on the proof." In his seminal text *Influence: The Psychology of Persuasion,* Robert Cialdini notes, "Once a stand is taken, there is a natural tendency to behave in way that is stubbornly consistent with the stand." What he means is that after someone has given mental assent to a view, they are going naturally to behave in ways to reinforce that view.

Any married couple is no doubt aware that once one partner has stated an opinion ("I know which way we're going"), it's extremely difficult to convince them of the contrary position. Once the initial opinion has been expressed, the challenge is even stronger, thanks to something known as confirmation bias. Confirmation bias causes us to look for and assign greater importance to information that supports our thesis.

In investing, consistency with a proposition and confirmation bias can be toxic to investment outcomes. If we develop an investment thesis and then look only for evidence to support its veracity, there is a significant danger of staying in bad investments too long, or worse, staying in them permanently as the business declines to zero.

A common solution to this dilemma that has been well documented to mitigate its effects is a process known as a *premortem*. A premortem is like a postmortem but is completed before the investment is made. The idea is to thoughtfully articulate all the possible ways that the investment could go wrong and then determine if there are any mitigants to those risks. It is a helpful way to surface potential issues. The premortem process was made popular by research psychologist Gary Klein. I would encourage a quick Google search for a working paper called "Rendering a Powerful Tool Flaccid: The Misuse of Premortems on Wall Street." In it, Klein, along with two equity portfolio managers, walk through the best way to implement a premortem process.

Managing Complexity—Checklists

"Fools ignore complexity," says computer scientist Alan Perlis. "Pragmatists suffer it. Some can avoid it. Geniuses remove it." Certainly, noted surgeon and *New Yorker* contributor Atul Gawande has done a significant amount to advocate for increased use of checklists. What Gawande and others have found is that in a world that is marked by increased specialization and increased levels of complexity, there is simply too much of a cognitive load for someone to try and keep in working memory all the things that need to be done.

Gawande, in his 2007 *New Yorker* article "The Check-list," tells the story of Peter Pronovost, a physician who worked to see checklists deployed in medical facilities. In one facility, checklists deployed to maintain proper sanitation procedures in intensive care units saw infection rates fall 66 percent in only three months. In the first eighteen months of the checklist program, $175 million in costs and 1,500 lives were saved.

Numbers such as these seem so large as to be almost misleading or potentially invalid. After all, how can something as simple as a list of *do-this, don't do that* drive such outcomes? The reality of medical practice is that in the hustle of the hospital/clinical setting, many things simply get overlooked, such as handwashing. Moreover, in many cases, repetition dulls the mind and leads to an inability to recall if you have followed all the proper procedures.

Investing is really no different: businesses, industries, and economies are highly complex entities. With public companies, specifically, there are numerous potential risk factors that could lead to an unfavorable investment outcome, which must all be taken into consideration. For example, an investor needs to understand how and why a customer purchases a given company's product, how the internal operations of the company function, how much debt the company carries and its appropriateness, what the regulatory environment is like, etc.

For each potential investment, there are numerous questions that must be answered and well understood to ensure that an appropriate assessment is made of the business. In my experience, there are simply too many things that need to be analyzed to keep them all in mind, which is the reason why an investment checklist is such a powerful tool.

Avoiding Error—Write-ups/ Process Improvement

"Any man can make mistakes, but only an idiot persists in his error," declared Marcus Tullius Cicero. That's why the third and critical pitfall we face as investors is error avoidance. Error avoidance comes from a shift in thinking, best thought of as process-versus-outcome thinking. In many areas of life, people focus entirely on outcomes. For example, "Did our team win or lose today?" With an outcome-based approach, when victory is attained, the feedback is to just continue to do the same thing and keep winning—don't fix what isn't broken. However, in a probabilistic environment such as investing, where many factors, including luck, can determine whether or not you're successful, uncovering why you were or were not successful is of the greatest importance. Focus on the process and the outcomes will be better and more consistent.

It's counterintuitive, but the greatest investment error one can make is when an investment works out favorably but not for the anticipated reasons. In that scenario, we are equally as wrong as when we make a bad investment but we don't receive the painful reminder that comes with a bad investment. Only by defining a robust investment process, where the reasons for making an investment decision are specifically documented, can this error be avoided over time. Finally, upon the completion of an investment, conducting a postmortem analysis is a valuable final step.

This analysis takes the original thesis and compares the outcome achieved with the original thinking. Were we right for the right reasons? This comparison provides the traceability to ensure that an investment was correct for the correct reasons. Where specific errors can be identified, this allows us to generate new checklist items and/or to further improve our investment write-up template.

I believe the end result of these steps to be an investment process that is self-reinforcing in nature. By using written analyses and postmortems the investment process itself becomes iterative (that is, it learns and grows over time) and we are able to improve over time by cultivating best practices from successful investments and learning from mistakes made. Checklists and a premortems help us to make sure that from the outset we are not letting things slip through the cracks (managing complexity) or neglecting to objectively analyze each investment. Compounding capital over time is demonstrably easier by avoiding losses in the first place.

When to Sell

In *Reminiscences of a Stock Operator,* journalist Edwin Le-Fevre writes, "You cannot always sell out when you wish or when you think it wise. You have to get out when you can; when you have a market that will absorb your entire line. Failure to grasp the opportunity to get out may cost you millions. You cannot hesitate."

The final step of investing is the art of the sell and the discipline required for it—knowing when to exit an investment. As we noted earlier, the actual process of making the decision to invest is largely brushed over analytically. In our experience, the process to follow when exiting a position is also given little consideration by investors.

During my time in investment research, I often encountered the commonsense wisdom of "You never go broke taking a profit" or "Pigs get fat, but hogs get slaughtered." The implication being that if you've made a profit, it almost always makes sense to exit your investment. The saying attributed to George Soros—"It takes courage to be a pig"—may have been tossed around as a contrarian retort to these sentiments. Rather than make intuition-based decisions using such commonsense refrains, we find it much more prudent to make decisions using a framework that has been thoroughly constructed in advance.

We believe the best place to begin evaluating the end of the investment (that is, the exit) is at the beginning (well before you've made the investment). Prudent investing, if it is to be more than gambling or a coin toss, involves first articulating a specific investment thesis. This thesis clearly describes what the investor believes will happen to the investment being evaluated. It should define in advance what catalysts are going to move shares, an approximate timeframe, and the risks and rewards present.

The well-defined investment thesis protects you from stumbling into Alice's quandary in Lewis Carroll's *Alice's Adventures in Wonderland* when she encounters the Cheshire Cat.

> *"Would you tell me, please, which way I ought to go from here?"*
>
> *"That depends a good deal on where you want to get to."*
>
> *"I don't much care where —"*
>
> *"Then it doesn't matter which way you go."*

If you never bother to define a specific investment thesis in advance of investing, you risk not knowing what the correct path forward is as circumstances develop. A well-defined investment thesis constructs a sell-discipline in advance, and is prescriptive about how to manage the investment as time progresses and circumstances develop.

Investment Scenarios

At the risk of stating the obvious, there are **four** potential outcomes to an actively managed investment:

→ **Correct decision:** The thesis is correct and the stock rises.

→ **Incorrect decision:** The thesis is incorrect and the stock falls.

→ **Lucky decision:** The thesis is incorrect yet the stock rises (for unexpected reasons).

→ **Unlucky decision:** The thesis is correct yet the stock falls.

Graphically, we can represent this as a simple two by two matrix (see Exhibit 10.2). Let's consider each scenario and offer a few thoughts about how best to handle each.

		STOCK PERFORMANCE	
		Stock Rises	Stock Falls
Thesis	Correct	Correct Decision	Unlucky Decision
	Incorrect	Lucky Decision	Incorrect Decision

EXHIBIT 10.2

Scenario 1. Exiting the Correct Decision

This may be the clearest of all the scenarios in that the investment performance has corroborated your thesis based on the specific catalysts you described in advance. As part of your investment thesis, you should define what you think the upside potential is (reward) to a downside case assessment of where the stock could go (risk). At the beginning of an investment, typically you want to see more upside potential than downside (reward over risk). The reason is we want to be compensated greater than one for each single unit of risk we're assuming.

By insisting on this scenario, we hope we're skewing the return potential of each idea and the portfolio itself in an asymmetric fashion (that is, this deliberate skewing of the portfolio is designed to disproportionately reward the investor versus the risk assumed). For example, why would we accept 50 percent upside potential versus 50 percent downside risk (that is, one times upside to downside) if there is another investment offering 50 percent upside but only 25 percent downside (that is, two times upside to downside)?

Scenario 2. Exiting the Incorrect Decision

Bernard Baruch, a remarkable investor of the 1920s, famously said,

> "Learn how to take losses quickly and cleanly. Don't expect to be right all the time. If you have a mistake, cut your losses as quickly as possible." And in *What I Learned Losing a Million Dollars,* Jim Paul and Brendan Moynihan tell us, "Market losses are external, objective losses. It's only when you internalize the loss that it

becomes subjective. This involves your ego and causes you to view it in a negative way, as a failure, something that is wrong or bad. Since psychology deals with your ego, if you can eliminate ego from the decision-making process, you can begin to control the losses caused by psychological factors."

As an investment develops, circumstances may arise that contradict the drivers of the investment thesis. When this occurs, we believe that an incorrect decision has been made. When your thesis is incorrect and the stock reflects this, the best course of action is a quick and speedy exit. In this situation, your reasons for being involved are no longer valid.

Many investors who do not define a specific investment thesis in advance have fallen victim to *thesis creep*—a debilitating affliction whereby the thesis for the investment is changing day by day with the direction of the market ("Of course, we bought Netflix because we saw the growth potential in Europe!"). Although it's certainly fatalistic to joke about how much worse something could get, we have seen that when companies begin to struggle, the near-term downside case can always be greater than anticipated. As such, it's best and prudent to exit and move on.

All good investors will be wrong on occasion and have losses; otherwise, you likely are not taking enough risk. More important is what's done after the loss. That's what determines long-term investment success.

Scenario 3. Exiting the Lucky Decision

Exiting the lucky decision is actually more difficult than exiting the incorrect decision in which your thesis was wrong and the stock went down. In scenario 3, you were just as wrong about your thesis, but you made money, which provides a tremendous psychological reward. Lest the surge of dopamine lead you to become overconfident about your abilities, a quick and timely exit is in order here as well. Again, this is another scenario in which an analysis after the investment will help you determine the underlying drivers of your success or failure.

Scenario 4. The Unlucky Decision

Handling the unlucky decision is the hardest of the four to navigate accurately. Inevitably in any investing, you're going to experience wide swings in a stock's price. In looking at the moves between the fifty-two-week highs and lows for stocks, it's quite common to see share price swings of 40 percent or more.

The point is it can be tough to tell at the time whether or not the investment decision was a bad one or just poorly timed (that is, unlucky). The recently reissued book *What I Learned Losing a Million Dollars* summarizes this situation well. Authors Paul and Moynihan note that the stock market is unique in that there is typically "no predetermined ending point" when making an investment. If you were to look at a betting scenario, for example on a sports event, it's clear when the game is over and the balance is to be settled. Conversely, a purchased stock can be held for years or in perpetuity with no determination necessarily being made with regard to the success or failure of the decision.

So what can be done? Paul and Moynihan offer some instructive thoughts. Note they use the term *speculation* here to mean any purchase made which you do not tend to hold until maturity (or, for stocks, hold indefinitely). "Speculation is forethought. And thought before action implies reasoning before a decision is made about what, whether, and when to buy or sell. That means the speculator develops several possible scenarios of future events and determines what his actions will be under each scenario. He thinks before he acts. Before you decide to get into the market you have to decide where (price) or when (time) or why (new information) you will no longer want the position."

As part of the initial analysis, Paul and Moynihan recommend specifying in advance when you want to sell. This *ex ante* decision unlocks the key to knowing how to handle the stock that goes down but has not given a sign that your investment thesis is incorrect. Defining in advance the rubric by which the stock is going to be judged against whether it is right or wrong, allows the investor to dispassionately evaluate the stock in the event of an unfortunate decline, instead of reacting emotionally to the pullback in shares.

As the stock moves around due to new information
and changes in the business, the investor can engage in a
sensible re-underwriting process that compares the new information and changes to the original thesis and catalysts
and determine if the *exit thresholds* have been breached. If
they have not, a pullback in value may present a wonderful
buying opportunity.

So for the unlucky decision, there is no hard and fast
rule about when to exit. Instead, it's going to be defined in
advance and is particular to each individual company.

Selecting an Investment Advisor

For most, investment will be a service that is procured on
the open market from one of a wide variety of possible ven-
dors. Very few individuals will choose to make wealth management a full-time occupation. With this being the most
likely state of affairs, it's important to outline some general
thoughts about how best to choose an investment advisor.

First, even if you decide to go down that path of working with a professional advisor, that does not negate the importance of our discussion to this point. In my experience
across the capital markets, the best client/advisor relationships occur where there is a strong alignment for how the
assets are to be managed. By walking through the development of a basic philosophy of investment and then understanding at a high level how sensible investment decisions

are made, you'll enter the process of selecting a professional advisor well equipped.

Before beginning, there are a few caveats to keep in mind. *First, how people are compensated drives behavior in the industry.* Financial services employees are, no surprise, highly economic creatures. Their compensation program and its inherent advantages and conflicts of interest will be a powerful determinate of their relationship with you as a client.

Second, the industry has different standards of care. Not all investment firms are fiduciaries—that is, required by law to put your interests ahead of their own. Those who are not fiduciaries are held to a *suitability* standard, that is, they cannot recommend something that's blatantly inappropriate for you. In my experience, I would generally choose a fiduciary advisor ahead of others. Regardless, you need to keep your eyes wide open about how the firm is compensated and any potential conflicts of interest.

Third, the team you land with means everything. Even at the largest and most august of institutions, you'll be working day in and day out with a particular team. How you interact with that team will be a key determinate in your ultimate satisfaction with you advisor. Most important, although the most slick and polished will be involved in the sales process, find ways to get in front of the people who will be involved with servicing your account day in and out.

How to Choose

The first step in choosing which advisor to partner with is determining what services you actually need to pay for. The financial services business, like any other, has a broad range of offerings. It's important to understand at the outset what the choices are and what yours and possibly your family's desires are if there is a larger group investing—in the case of a family business, for example. Let's consider a few options.

Investment Consultant. One possible option in investing is to hire a pure investment consultant. An investment consultant typically charges a modestly lower fee because they only make recommendations, as opposed to taking on management (also termed taking on discretion) of the investment accounts. The investment consultant space generally began to provide advisory services to the pension community and the board of directors who oversee pensions assets.

Because they serve as a consultant only, the classic knock against consultants is that they will do whatever they can to keep the business. Just as "no one gets fired for hiring IBM," in general, consultants are known for largely conventional advice. Even if they're recommending specific investment managers, I would argue that you'll find a recommended slate that is as close to the middle of the fairway as possible.

That being said, there are several consulting firms that have built excellent relationships with the private wealth space. And because consultants work with numerous clients across a wide base of client types, they'll generally be in the know about emerging trends and where consensus is. I've also found several consulting firms to have quite robust reporting capabilities, which help investment-performance benchmarking.

Keep in mind as well that consultants can be generalists or highly specialized. Even if you decide a generalist team is not the right choice, a private equity or hedge fund specialist might be incredibly helpful in identifying interesting managers, as well as assisting in the due diligence process.

Asset Manager. If you want a partner who will take over management of the assets one possibility is to go directly to an asset manager. An asset manager is generally in the primary business of managing assets, usually for institutional clients. This is important because they are not going to be staffed well enough to provide higher-touch client services like financial planning, multigenerational education, etc.

Nevertheless, because they compete in a diverse and large marketplace, pricing in the space is well known and highly competitive. You'll generally find the lowest and best pricing here, especially if you look at global firms like Blackrock, which may have trillions of dollars in assets under management.

This transparency around pricing and competitive markets also will help to provide you with a much-needed barometer for the cost of the additional services you may receive at other institutions. For example, if you know that you're paying 0.25 percent (that is, twenty-five basis points—a basis point is one one-hundredth of a percent), if you get a proposal back from a multi-family office for services at 0.75 percent basis points, you can reasonably surmise that additional fifty basis points are going to cover the additional family office services.

Large Financial Institution. The next option would be to consider working with a large-scale financial institution. These institutions may also be in the asset-management business, which can make separating them from the categories above more challenging. Large financial institutions typically have more than $10 billion in assets under management. There are a few major subtypes to highlight.

- ➜ *Banks.* Large banking institutions may have a *private wealth* or *family office* offering that they hold out to select clients who meet a higher minimum in assets. Common examples here would include JP Morgan Private Banking and Citi Private Banking. They offer a broad range of services including asset management along with specialty lending, credit cards, etc.

- ➜ *Trust institutions.* Large trust institutions (also termed *trust banks*) derived from some of the earliest family offices of the Robber Baron era. Common example here would include Northern Trust, Bessemer Trust, Brown Brothers Harriman, and

Glenmede Trust. Many of these firms are close to 100 years old or older, and have deep experience in working with the needs of wealthy families. One common differentiator is how open their investment platforms are and whether or not they manage the majority of assets internally or not.

➤ ***Brokerages.*** Brokerage firms will have a separate tier known as private wealth, private client, or family office for their highest-net-worth clients. Common examples here would include Goldman Sachs Private Wealth Management and BNY Mellon.

➤ ***Multi-Family Offices.*** Multi-family offices (MFOs) often begin as single-family offices and then expand to other clients to help leverage the cost invested in building the platform. They are a rapidly growing slice of the investment-management world. If you begin to explore working with an MFO, it's important to understand what services are being offered and what you're paying for.

Because MFOs often advertise themselves as a one-stop shop, it's worth understanding what they mean by that. For example, with something like in-house legal counsel, it's important to understand the relationship you will have with outside counsel and who will be drafting documents. In my experience, with ongoing changes in trust law and litigation experience, it remains of critical importance to have a legal partner who is well versed in current trust and estates practices.

Investment acumen is also worth diving into with an MFO. MFOs come into existence in a variety of ways and may have legacy expertise in accounting or tax, but their investment platform may be subpar. I would recommend a more thorough conversation with their investment team about the platform, manager-selection process, and how ideas come in and out of client portfolios. It's also important to understand whether you will have a separate account or be in a pooled vehicle (separate limited partnership or common trust fund), which is true for whomever you decide to work with.

→ *Local Firms.* Finally, in every city there are likely a small number of local firms that may be worth talking to. There are trade-offs, of course, to being with a smaller, more local institution. Do you want to be a big fish in a small pond? Are they sophisticated enough to handle your needs? These are two key questions to consider. That being said, if you're at the top of a fifteen-to-twenty client local or regional firm, you're likely to find excellent service from a team that is earnest to keep your business. Investment sophistication, though, may be a drag on performance since many local firms may have little experience or sophistication in building complex asset allocations or in evaluating the unique private assets that larger sums of money have access to.

The Final Decision

Now that you have sense of the possible options, it's important to meet with at least three or four candidates. Even if you've had a relationship in place for a number of years, it can be worth re-evaluating your current provider in light of your new circumstances. The additional feedback you get from other firms, along with the new insight you may gain into the operations of your current firm, will likely reinvigorate the relationship you have in place.

Having sat in many prospecting meetings and completed scores of proposals, I offer a few thoughts about how best to manage a selection process. First, the more information you can provide at the outset, the better. Having up-to-date statements, records of other investments, even insurance policies, available with copies to share will help the firm you're speaking with customize their conversation to your particular circumstances.

Unless you do this, you're likely to get a generic boilerplate speech, but it's not going to be more robust than the cursory information you're able to find on the firm's website. Instead, by priming the pump with additional information, you'll be able to see the firm's best thinking on your circumstances and priorities.

As you enter into those conversations, there are three things you should be trying to evaluate:

First, people. Investment advisory is ultimately a business of trust and people. Understanding how well you get along with the team is paramount. Meeting the rest of the client-service team, not just the sales professionals, is important. Asking for references as you get further down the process is a good step—and even better if you can use your own contacts to locate a reference.

Understanding the team's average client and how you stand relative to them. If you're too big, the team may not be ready to service your needs. If you're too small, you'll find your customer service slipping over time or the firm will find other creative ways to generate additional income from your accounts.

The firm itself. The nature of the firm, its ownership, and how team members are compensated will have a powerful influence on the type of service you receive. If the firm is not a registered investment advisor or trust company, diving into the question of fiduciary versus suitability will be key to understanding any conflicts of interest that may be present, and going eyes-wide-open into any transaction.

Technology and reporting are important as well. Ask to see a sample report. Is it easy to understand? Is your performance presented net of fees and is it easy to compare to relevant benchmarks? Beware of performance presentations that are *gross of fees*. I've seen some egregious attempts to inflate the performance shown to a client. And inquire as to what the client portal is like and how easy it is to access.

Understanding fees is of course important. I would encourage you to recognize that fees are largely negotiable, depending on the firm. As well, fees are common knowledge in the industry. Fee schedules are disclosed at least annually through the investment advisor registration process with the SEC and are available in the firm's ADV document. Many investment consultants publish fee surveys of the industry.

The investment process. Each firm will have different ways to invest, and it's important that their view aligns with your thoughts and responses to the questions outlined earlier in this chapter. For individuals, focusing on tax efficiency of portfolios is a key differentiator. Having the manager walk through how frequently they trade, their typical capital gains/losses annually, and even average capital gains distributions from mutual funds held in your account will tell you a lot about what the true cost of the service rendered.

Performance. I did not highlight performance as a key portion of the conversation. The simple reality is that it's very difficult to get accurate, complete, and transparent performance data from a firm. Each client has unique circumstances that impact performance, for example, low-basis stock from a company that went public.

The natural incentive is for firms to find ways to show their best numbers. Many times this means that try to show only certain accounts, rather than all accounts that would be similar in strategy to yours. If you do ask about performance, you should look for that performance to be calculated in accordance with the Global Investment Performance Standards (GIPS); if it is not in compliance, you should expect to see disclosures. GIPS is a defined protocol for calculating and presenting performance, which takes into account common ways that firms play games with the performance figures.

How to Invest Poorly

Thus far in this chapter we have covered how to invest if you are seeking positive long-term returns. For the balance of the chapter, we consider the inverse, exploring how not to invest and where the wealthy often go wrong.

Firing the Bad Money Manager

The data is conclusive that the average investor has historically done abysmally poorly versus the broader market indices. As Exhibit 10.1 highlights, while the S&P 500 has generated a 6.1 percent annualized since 1999, and a more blended 60 percent equity/40 percent bond portfolio produced 5.6 percent annually, the average investor has generated only 1.9 percent.

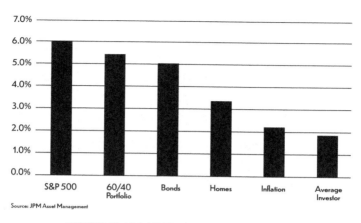

Source: JPM Asset Management

**EXHIBIT 10.1 20-YEAR ANNUALIZED RETURNS
BY ASSET CLASS (1999-2019)**

So the question is why is the individual investor missing out so regularly? It seems unnecessary to say but the goal is to buy low and sell high and not the reverse. Yet, over-whelmingly the data shows that investors do just the opposite. Investors, both individual and institutional, tend to follow the herd, by buying in and staying too long in the best-performing asset classes, and not buying what is cheap.

The driver for this in its simplest form is our own brain chemistry. When stocks are going up and we're making money, our brains reward us with a lot of positive dopamine. The reverse is true when stocks are falling. As such, rather than thinking with our risk-management hats on, we tend to think in terms of gain and loss. When we experience losses, we're less likely to behave rationally and tend to hold our losers far too long.

A second way that bad investment behavior manifests is in buying and selling too much. The average investor trades too frequently and misses out on performance through the mistiming. Studies also show that when investors choose to terminate relationships with underperforming investment managers, it's almost always right before their performance begins to recover. The only way to mitigate this is through a robust investment process so that performance is evaluated relative to the inputs to the numbers (that is, how the manager makes investment decisions) and not the outputs (that is, the returns generated). It sounds counterintuitive but it's true.

The combination of these behavioral challenges hurts investors ability to stay in the market long enough to generate good returns, or avoid significant drawdowns by rebalancing when assets classes have become too expensive.

A New Way to Think About Investing

Those who become wealthy through the ownership of a business must keep in mind that capital allocation within a business is very different from capital allocation in the markets. In his letter to Berkshire Hathaway shareholders in 1987, Warren Buffet writes: "Many individuals come into wealth by serving as owners/managers of businesses. There are very distinct differences in allocating capital within a company and within an investment portfolio." Let's compare and contrast the two approaches.

How CEOs Invest

Shortly after initiating coverage of my first company as a sell-side equity research analyst, I attended a client dinner with the company's management team. Over the course of the meal, the CFO pulled me aside to ask my opinion of a recently announced share repurchase program. The situation was unique, since the company had only recently gone public, presumably to raise needed funds for investment, and here they were a year later, admitting they had no other opportunities for investment in their business, except for buying back their own shares. The question raised by this CFO is one heard frequently from both investors and from senior executives at the companies we interact with: *What do I do with my capital?* This is among the most pressing and frankly career-defining choices that a senior executive team for a company can wrestle with.

As Warren Buffett noted in his 1987 letter to shareholders, at a firm that retains 10 percent of its earnings over a ten-year period, the CEO will be responsible for allocating almost two-thirds of the total capital at work in the business. We would argue that a 10 percent retention rate is quite low for most businesses, so the stakes are even higher. So for those who think CEOs are not investors, think again.

There are four key tools that support successful capital allocation by a CEO. First, these managers had a strong capital-tracking discipline in place. Although finance theory and business schools teach managers to invest only in projects where the IRR (returns) exceeds the WACC (cost of capital), we often wonder how many managers actually track the returns of their projects on a one-year, five-year, or ten-year basis? The first step to allocating capital well is having the systems and processes in place to measure the effectiveness of capital allocation. Just as public market investors have regular updates on the performance of their portfolio, companies should rigorously review and assess the returns generated from their investments. The natural temptation in business is to always be moving forward, fighting the next fire, chasing the next deal, launching the next product, etc. The task of retrospection must always be viewed in light of Santayana's wise maxim, "Those who cannot remember the past are condemned to repeat it."

Second, managers must have a strong understanding of the reinvestment characteristics of their business. A CEO is faced with two primary decisions regarding capital allocation—to either add more capital to the business or return capital to shareholders. The choice between each must be driven by a sober assessment of the industry dynamics in which they participate.

Those who work in a single industry, and especially those who have never left that industry, run the very real risk of having blinders on with regard to the characteristics of their own industry. All the reinvestment in the world is going to be hard pressed to generate incremental value in highly competitive industries with little strategic differentiation. We see this constantly in capital-intensive, cyclical industries, where companies add capacity at the top of the cycle. Take, for example, the cement or gypsum wallboard industries here in the U.S. In these industries, managements consistently overestimate the likely future profitability of their industry and destroy shareholder value by overinvesting at the peak of the cycle.

Third, these CEOs sized their balance sheets and debt profiles conservatively and appropriately to their business model. There is a level of debt appropriate to each business model, and it's largely a function of the return characteristics of the business, the volatility of the cash flow stream, and the cyclicality of the industry in which it participates. By running at appropriate leverage (debt/EBITDA or cash flow) levels, the company is protected from the vagaries of the marketplace, and never finds itself in a position of being forced to raise capital. Just like a loan shark, the institutional credit market takes its pound of flesh when capital is least available and is most needed.

Finally, they knew the value of their own stock. Too many public company CEOs and CFOs do not know how to sensibly value their own company. You see this with management teams that repurchase shares when the company's stock is making new highs, but are suspiciously inactive when shares are hitting new lows (ideally, the timing of their actions would be the reverse).

The value of a business is simply what a sensible buyer is willing to pay for the stream of cash flows your business can be expected to generate. How do you discern this value? Why not pick up the phone and talk with some of your long-term investors and deep dive into how they think about valuing their business? This is not the time to quibble about valuation multiples or models, but a time to understand what a rational, long-term holder is willing to pay.

These are the challenges for management teams who have complete and total information to accurately make a decision about their own stock. For those who were formerly management teams and are now tasked with investing their own capital, the tension is even worse. When you're running a company and it's growing, you look across your various business opportunities and determine which opportunities warrant more resources and capital to support and perhaps even further accelerate their growth. It's a feed-your-winners mentality. If one department or product line grew 20 percent last year, maybe it can grow 25 percent next year if we give it an additional $20 million of investment.

How *Investors* Invest

The manner by which you invest in public stocks is the inverse of how capital is invested within an operating business. A friend and smart investor, who used to serve as the chief investment officer for a family office, and I were discussing investing one day and he highlighted this principle as one of his largest struggles in working with the family. As business owners take stock at the end of the year, we see what businesses and divisions did well. We then engage in a capital-budgeting process and as we prioritize where to spend our limited capital, it only makes sense to want to continue to invest in what is already doing well. When families begin to invest in the markets, they look not at what has done well but at what has done poorly or lagged. Such sectors may hold opportunity that the market has not recognized yet.

Families must recognize that they are now participants in an efficient market. When an operating company is owned and controlled out right, the owners have access to several unique market inefficiencies. They likely have sources of non-public information about suppliers, customers, and competitors. These sources can be combined in novel ways to drive new product development, operational efficiencies, or even M&A strategy. As an outside investor, this efficiency goes away. In the case of investments in public companies, management teams are highly regulated in the data they can and cannot share with their shareholder base.

This is because there is an additional step present as an external versus internal investor. As an internal investor, you effectively get to buy wholesale. You see what it costs to invest in growth with no additional mark up. If the returns warrant the risk incurred, you open the new store, install the additional manufacturing line, etc. On the public side, as an external investor, there is an additional price being added to the wholesale price. So rather than buying wholesale, the wholesale price is being escalated by the market's opinion of the value of the future cash flows the growth will lead to.

Even in the case of buying private companies, with the number of private equity funds, sovereign wealth funds, search funds, and other family offices actively searching for, pursuing due diligence, and closing on deals in an industry, there are a host of people who are being engaged to find relevant information that can be used to add returns to the business. Because of the number of other bidders and limited information available, this leads to the creation of a market. As such, the potential for outsized returns (especially versus a diversified benchmark like the S&P 500) is greatly reduced. The price being paid for the business is highly likely to reflect both the current economic reality of the business, as well as likely pathways for additional value creation.

Second, families must recognize that their capital-allocation decisions are infinitely broader now. Earlier in my career, when I was moving from an analyst to a portfolio manager, one of the key things I learned was that just because a specific company is the best opportunity in its industry (that is, the view of an industry-focused analyst), the determination a portfolio manager must make is whether it's the best opportunity relative to all other competing options (that is, cross-industries).

For years, a family-owned company has had its choices regarding capital allocation nicely constrained. They could either reinvest in the operating business through capital expenditures or M&A, or they could return capital to shareholders through dividends/share repurchase. The re-investment decision is largely binary. Now, as an investor, the family can consider a global range of options across a plethora of asset classes. This dramatically increases the complexity of the choice architecture—which may necessitate the need for additional team members, education for the family, and new advisors to assist in the process.

Warning: Investments Are Generally Sold, Not Bought

Finally, families must recognize and resist the story-driven nature of investing. To an outsider, investing appears to be a largely quantitative practice. But I can definitively say that the most advanced math I've ever used in my investment career is algebra, with an occasional bit of statistics thrown in. Instead, investing, at its core, is the analysis of a situation and then the creation of a narrative about the opportunity and future potential ahead. Whether in equity research or investment banking, this is the fundamental task that those professionals are engaged in.

This matters to families because those employed in the production of financial products are really quite good at telling stories. They can craft narratives that appeal to your emotions, greed, hubris, etc., in order to get a transaction done, simply because they are ultimately compensated by their ability to get someone to act. As such, families must be on guard as they evaluate those stories to find the true sources of long-term opportunity. This is best done by insisting that investing be executed in the same way the family ran its manufacturing facilities—in a process-oriented, methodical, and measured way that will help mitigate the emotional appeal of a great story.

Conclusion

For most, the investment component of a wealth strategy will be the largest use of funds. Whether due to complexity or psychology, though, oftentimes investors give very little consideration to how they will go about their investment affairs. In this chapter, we have considered the core elements that undergird any successful, long-term investment approach. We covered risk and how to think about losses. We next considered the importance of defining an investment philosophy that considers your views of the market itself and how one might go about outperforming it. We next considered how to implement investment decisions—when to buy, when to sell, and how to improve your investment process. We concluded by looking at how to hire an investment advisor and how investment mistakes are often made. Admittedly, despite this being the book's longest chapter, we have only scratched the surface of all these topics. If you are interested in learning more, I offer a few suggestions for additional reading.

Books to Consider

Family Capital, Greg Curtis

Winning the Loser's Game, Charles Ellis

What I Learned Losing a Million Dollars, Jim Paul and Brendan Moynihan

The Essays of Warren Buffett, Lawrence Cunningham and Warren Buffett

Against the Gods: The Remarkable Story of Risk, Peter Bernstein

How Smart People Make Big Money Mistakes, Gene Belsky and Thomas Gilovich

Fooling Some People All the Time, David Einhorn

When Genius Failed, Roger Lowenstein

CHAPTER 10

GIVING TO THE NEXT GENERATION

"I must study politics and war, that our sons may have liberty to study . . . commerce and agriculture, in order to give their children a right to study . . . poetry . . ."

—JOHN QUINCY ADAMS

I t's nearly a universal truth that at a certain age, everyone's thinking begins to shift from their own life to the life beyond. Perhaps, as the time horizon of one's life shortens, the present reality of one's mortality becomes ever more apparent. In this shift, considerations surrounding legacy are no longer just theoretical in nature. Just last week, I sat with a couple in their mid-sixties. Although they were early in their retirement years, they'd seen two close friends lose their fight with cancer, and the uncertainty and lack of guarantee of the days ahead were pushing them to begin to articulate their wishes for beyond the grave.

The choices involved in one's passing can be numerous in the short term. Where does one want to be interred? Or perhaps cremated? I had one grandparent who accumulated almost a dozen burial plots over the years, perhaps in hopes that the family would all chose to be buried together. But over the course of time, the family had all moved away from its geographic origin. Yet once those practical considerations are addressed, a shift begins as to what happens to the money and what happens to the stuff.

How Much Is Too Much to Give?

As parents and grandparents this is one of the seminal questions we must all answer. Sadly, like many values-related questions that surface around money, there is no clear answer. Like Justice Potter Stewart, in his famous remark about obscenity, "I know it when I see it," we all possess some sense of how much is too much when it comes to giving money to future generations. Tabloid coverage of Paris Hilton years ago, the "Rich Kids of Instagram," and tales of other trust fund brats rest heavily on our minds as something to avoid.

We see two typical responses to the question of how much. One is a passive response: Either *I cannot tell my children no* or *I haven't given it much thought.* The other is an excessively controlling one: trust documents/structures that define the 900 possible categories for when a trust distribution is or is not appropriate. But neither approach provides a satisfactory answer to the question of how much. The passive approach can lead to entitlement, frustration, or a lack of direction. The controlling approach can lead to the opposite of what was intended.

One survey of 3,250 affluent families conducted by two trust-and-estate advisors (Preisser and Williams) showed that over 70 percent of estates become unglued after estate transitions. Meaning trust structures are unwound through probate litigation or other means, rendering all the structures outlined moot. And 90-95 percent of advisors are changed after an estate transition. So even for structures that stay in place, the advisors who knew the benefactors best and their values/philosophies are not going to be around to oversee implementation of the trust structure.

So of the 70 percent, why did they fail? Ninety-five percent of the time, the actual plan was correct from a legal/tax perspective. Only 2-3 percent of failures were due to issues with the advice rendered. As Preisser and Williams noted, the assets were being prepared for heirs, and not the other way around.

Preparing the Heirs for the Assets

How can we more thoroughly address preparing the heirs for the assets—as we prepare the assets for the heirs? As we read in Roald Dahl's *Charlie and the Chocolate Factory,* "Don't forget what happened to the man who suddenly got everything he wanted," says Mr. Wonka. "What happened?" says Charlie Bucket. "He lived happily ever after." With no offense to Mr. Dahl, this is rarely the outcome. Seventy-five percent of business owners who sell their business say they are unhappy with the decision twelve months after sale. And 80 percent of individuals with a trust fund say that it has been a negative influence in their lives.

For most, wealth serves three primary functions. First, it serves a defensive function, as it provides protection against the various unforeseen negative circumstances that arise in life. Second, it provides an easy score board for measuring one's success. Finally, money enables consumption and a certain standard of living.

Generally, as folks earn/receive/invest/spend financial resources, it's with one of those three contexts in mind. When we contemplate giving to others, it's likely due to a shift in financial posture. Perhaps it's obvious, but it's important to recognize: *If we can begin to give to others, it implies that we have more than enough to satisfy the three core functions—defense, consumption, and success.* This shift underlies the statistics mentioned earlier regarding the unhappiness of newly liquid business owners or trust fund beneficiaries.

As we reach a position of excess, the practical dollars and cents matter less, and the softer questions regarding values, legacy, and intention move to the forefront. Navigating those questions requires beginning to cultivate a legacy mindset.

At the outset, I think it's helpful to begin to address such a nebulous question by considering how you want your family to remember you at your funeral, one year after you're gone, and five years after. We discussed earlier the concept of eulogy virtues and those are of paramount importance in answering this question. Philanthropic advisory firm 21/64 has created a helpful deck of cards (Picture Your Legacy™ cards) about envisioning your legacy as a way to let pictures spark the process.

Next, having articulated your own values, consider your desire to see those values continue in the family. There is a fine line to walk here, because if you're too demanding in those values, you will be seen as ruling from the grave. But you may be able to use your legacy planning to support the continuation of those values.

Finally, what do you own that you want to keep in the family and why? For some families, this is a piece of land or a vacation property that has emotional or historical significance to you and the family. As the family grows (exponentially not linearly), keeping those assets in the family will grow more challenging. Finding a way to *endow* those assets will help ensure their place in the family going forward.

In thinking about how much to give to your children and grandchildren, author David York recommends "focusing on the flint and kindling" and not the fire. As I learned as a Boy Scout many years ago, starting a fire requires three key elements, a flint, a steel, and tinder/kindling. When making a fire without matches, the steel strikes the flint to create a spark. The spark is captured by the tinder/kindling and slowly fanned into a roaring fire.

In passing on wealth to future generations, the issue underlying the proverb of "shirtsleeves to shirtsleeves in three generations" is that future generations lose the ability to create wealth. That is, as the mentality shifts from creation of the family fortune, to tending to it, and ultimately to spending it. A different skill set is required to tend a fire than create one entirely.

Yet the reality of families and family fortunes is that the assets of the family have to grow at a high rate to benefit future generations. Between the ongoing impact of inflation, the multiplicative powers of procreation, and the negative impact of taxes, capital has to be compounded at a rate of at least 10 percent for each successive generation to receive a benefit similar in size to the generations that came before.

For closely held businesses, the forces of creative destruction are another risk. The primary assets that brought a family to wealth are simply not going to be able to sustain this growth rate into perpetuity in a competitive market economy. As such, the family must find new ways to grow and produce wealth, that is, fire starting, not fire tending.

Do not misinterpret my point, the fire tending of existing assets must be done well, with excellent corporate governance and sophisticated investment management. That effort is necessary but not sufficient for furthering the prosperity of a family. York's advice is to *focus on creating the spark and providing the necessary resources to catch the fire.*

As we think about giving to our kids, we should enquire of each gift *if it is going to create the spark.* Education and other chances to develop nascent gifts/talents are great sparks. If it's not a spark, is it providing the tinder to catch the spark? A modest amount of resources may enable the launch of a new entrepreneurial venture, or start a career that may have not been accessible without some financial assistance.

A quick disclaimer is warranted here. Within your family or in generations to come may be someone who has the desire, skills, and perseverance required to become a wealth creator. But for most of the family, their own personal paths toward a meaningful life likely won't include the path of entrepreneurship. So when providing flint and kindling, I would encourage you to recognize that the creative potential in future generations may be expressed differently.

Choosing Where to Step In

Author Lee Hausner uses the following categories to organize the various circumstances that a parent or grandparent could potentially assist with.

Life Stages
- Birth to age eighteen
- College years
- Early career
- Marriage/buying first house

Special Circumstances

→ Provide for handicapped child or grandchild

→ Health care needs

→ Other

As you consider each category, you may or may not feel that giving at that stage is appropriate, but it may help you articulate where your line in the sand is. For families of significant means, there are likely assets even beyond what categories they desire to fund. So the question that surfaces is what to do in this situation. Hausner offers four other possible categories that could be helpful to fund:

→ A family bank, for helping the family launch new ventures

→ An education trust, for funding the education of future generations

→ A family foundation, for supporting social causes important to the family

→ A legacy trust, for supporting the family's unity—regular gatherings, trips, etc.

Jay Hughes writes, "Where are the guideposts or roadmaps for someone for whom the question is not, 'How do I make a living?' but rather, 'Given that I have money, how do I live well?'" He develops the analogy that a gift of any sort can be like a meteor crashing into the world of the recipient, who then has to figure out how to integrate and possibly adjust their lifestyle. Gifts from one generation to another are in one sense the transfer of the wishes/hopes/

dreams of a prior generation to the next. The task of the recipient is to determine how best their own dreams align with those of the gifter.

When evaluating gifting strategy, take time to reflect and plan for life after the gift. First, assess the recipient of your gift. Are they ready to make the shift of mindset from working to make a living to determining what does a life well lived look like? Are you ready to serve as a guide along that path? Are you ready for the giving up of control that comes when an asset that was formerly yours now belongs to another?

Although none of us wants to pay taxes above and beyond what is owed, no one wants to hinder the potential of our children or grandchildren by failing to give well. Finally have the awkward conversation appropriately early and often. "Without open communication about social and emotional implications of having wealth," writes J.H. O'Neill in *The Golden Ghetto: The Psychology of Affluence,* "inheritors may feel ashamed of receiving handed-down wealth, guilt because they had so much, and inadequate when compared to the people in the family who made the fortune."

Of all the conversations I have with families and their advisors, when, how much detail, and how often to communicate about wealth are frequent questions. Invariably, this is an area of some sensitivity. In many cases, families do not want to reveal the full extent of the family's wealth at the risk of hurting the children and robbing them of the ability to achieve.

Conversely, I was struck recently in a conversation with a second-generation family member in a family of significant means. This individual had some suspicion of the family's wealth, but did not receive full disclosure until he was twenty-four and completing graduate school. The level of the family's wealth came crashing into her world for the first time, leading to a major reconsideration of her career choice and her responsibility to work within the family business. We cannot help but think that this individual would have been much better served through a series of progressive discussions detailing the family's holdings and the likely impact they would have on her own financial picture and professional aspirations.

Clearly, nuance is the name of the game here. A certain amount of disclosure that is age appropriate based on the child's developmental stage and emotional maturity is a beginning point. Certainly, in our experience, there is a time when it's important to begin the dialog of a more complete disclosure.

I say *begin* because all matters of great life importance take time to understand and digest, even more so when complex financial fortunes are involved. Certainly, great sensitivity and care must be given when children are inheriting at different levels than siblings, or perhaps not at all. Nevertheless, better to begin this sensitive dialog when the parent is present than risk the legacy of the relationship between parent and child by waiting until the reading of the will following the parent's passing.

What Happens to the Stuff?

In determining what to do when disposing of one's physical possessions, consider the legacy of David Rockefeller. Rockefeller was a tremendous collector of art and antiques. Upon his death, the vast majority of his possessions went to auction, with the nearly $1 billion in proceeds raised donated to charity.

The simple reality is that outside of a few items, your possessions are most likely just that—yours. The *New York Times* has documented recently the rapidly declining value of antiques as current generations choose more contemporary styles to decorate their homes. The self-storage industry exists entirely because families do not know how to move on with mom and dad's things. Rather than move on, families are stuck with a monthly bill to cover the storage of stuff they don't want. Don't stick future generations with more baggage to take through life and a monthly expense to cover it. Make the decision for them and as appropriate and move things on.

No doubt there are a few family heirlooms that the family will want to keep. Define in advance an equitable process to pass those items along. Draw straws and then take turns. Or name specifically whom certain items are to go to. Your eventual passing will be a stressful enough event, arousing suspicions, envy, and strife in the distribution of physical goods. Leaving questions unanswered is not the way to go in peace.

Living well in the context of one's financial means and values is no easy task. This challenge is magnified even further when we decide to share those means with successive generations. Taking the time to analyze and thoughtfully draft a wealth plan and then consider one's gifting intentions provides the framework necessary to build a robust and comprehensive estate plan and an accompanying investment strategy to support it. This chapter has purposefully been kept short for two reasons. First, estate-planning conversations can become exceedingly technical very quickly. The excellent lawyers and accountants who work in this field will be most up to date on specific techniques. Secondly, this is an area where, candidly, I think others have said it best. For most, assets given to the next generation will likely utilize some sort of trust structure. There are a tremendous number of considerations to keep in mind about the human implications of using trust structures. As you weigh those choices, I would commend *The Cycle of the Gift: Family Wealth and Wisdom,* by James E. Hughes, Susan Massenzio, and Keith Whitaker, as an excellent place to begin.

CHAPTER 11

PHILANTHROPY

"If you are perceived to have the ability to give away money,
everybody lies to you, always."

—ADVISOR TO THE ROCKEFELLER FAMILY

—

I f you've thoughtfully considered your consumption, as discussed in Chapter 9, "How to Spend It," and crafted a legacy plan for your assets, it's reasonable to assume there may be assets in your possession that are above and beyond what's needed to fund those priorities. Even on a year-in-year-out basis, we all face regular asks to support causes important to our friends, and likely have several causes of our own that we're passionate about supporting.

Let's consider next the question of what to do when you want to thoughtfully give wealth away. Knowing when and how to give is not easy. Early in his career, Warren Buffett believed it would be foolish to be philanthropic too early, given his ability to compound wealth. Admittedly, given the size of his later donations to the foundations run by his children and to the Bill and Melinda Gates Foundation, he made up for the delay in spades.

These difficult questions are ones that I've taken to heart over the last several years. I've read many books, re-read several other thoughtful articles, and scoured far and wide to find examples of thoughtful engagement in philanthropy. What follows is some of the feedback from these considerations, as well as a few of my own thoughts about this critical choice.

Philanthropy Always Begins with Consumption

Although it may not be popular to say it, philanthropy and the choice to give to others begins with first assessing how much is *enough* for you. In fact, I would argue that our level of philanthropy is an excellent indicator of our level of contentment, satisfaction, and gratitude in our lives.

That is why Chapter 9, about sensible consumption, came first in this book. Thoughtfully wrestling with and articulating a desired standard of living are important in how we consider philanthropy. That said, there is an important nuance to highlight. While consumption is ostensibly about building a life that makes us happy, it's important to recognize that philanthropy has a massively positive effect on our lives. Scientific studies have confirmed that generosity is strongly correlated with personal happiness. The same is true with the regular practice of gratitude. As such, consumption cannot rightfully be considered in isolation from the question of generosity. The two are closely intertwined. Consumption shows a declining marginal benefit above a certain level, whereas philanthropic work elevates one's happiness. From a mathematical perspective, if you were being completely self-interested, there is a point where consumption would cease growing and all additional funds would go immediately toward philanthropy.

Philanthropy and Legacy Are Intimately Connected

Consumption and self-actualization are tied to philanthropy. Indeed, more and more, individuals and families are discovering the powerful role that philanthropy serves in helping to refine and pass along the core values, identity, and their place in the history of the family. Across all the facets of strategically approaching wealth, families who find the greatest fulfillment and the greatest long-term success are those who take the time to articulate the history, values, and priorities of the family as they contemplate their desired legacy. From this background, they can thoughtfully engage with their trusted advisors to implement the goals that surface in that process.

So What Can We Learn From Previous Philanthropists?

Looking back, arguably the most thoughtful modern consideration of philanthropy is Andrew Carnegie's 1889 essay "Wealth." Interestingly, in today's economic climate of a growing void of economic inequality, Carnegie's words ring truer than ever.

Carnegie was quick to recognize the role that philanthropy plays in a democratic society.

> "The problem of our age is the proper administration of wealth, so that the ties of brotherhood may still bind together the rich and poor in harmonious relationship . . . there remains, then, only one mode of using great fortunes; but in this we have the true antidote for the temporary unequal distribution of wealth, the reconciliation of the rich and the poor—a reign of harmony. After doing so to consider all surplus revenues which come to him simply as trust funds, which he is called upon to administer, and strictly bound as a matter of duty to administer in the manner which, in his judgment, is best calculated to produce the most beneficial results for the community."

Bill Gates affirmed this view in 2007 during a speech at the Tech Museum of Innovation in San Jose, where he noted the unique role of philanthropy, "which can step in when market forces aren't doing the job." Both Gates and Carnegie see philanthropy as uniquely positioned to remedy the inherent failings of the capitalist system.

The Process for Effective Philanthropy

Great books have been written to answer the questions surrounding effective philanthropy, and I'll reference several at the close of this chapter. But it's at least worth outlining a high-level process to consider as you make your philanthropic commitments.

First, philanthropy begins through the identification of a challenge. Whether through your own due diligence or the appeal of another, you've been presented with a wrong in the world that you perceive needs to be righted. The scope of possibility here truly is endless. And so those who are serious about giving money away have to screen the possible choices for philanthropic investment the same way those who invest financial capital in pursuit of an investment return.

Following close behind the identification of a cause is a crucial step that is regularly overlooked because it's so implicit, which is the development and articulation of a theory of change. Put simply, what is the most effective way to address the issue that needs to be remedied.

For example, in the United States, there is a near unanimous consensus that our K-12 education system is inadequately equipped to support student and drive outcomes. Yet, if you were to discuss the issue with parents, teachers, administrators, community leaders, and elected officials, you would have as many unique possible solutions to the problem as people you spoke with. A theory of change is a thesis about where to start in addressing the problem. Selecting the right *theory of change* to fund is highly important. Making this selection accurately leads many charities to develop and provide regular updates on various metrics to measure the impact they're having in addressing their issue of specialty.

Of course, there are a couple of sizable challenges that can prohibit rendering an accurate verdict about the effectiveness of a theory of change. First, philanthropy, because it exists outside of an economic marketplace, does not receive the same information and signaling as those organizations that participate in a for-profit capacity.

When you're managing a company, the ability to set a price for a good or service and then see the reaction of market demand to that price will communicate to the management team whether they're on the right track. If the price is set too high, demand may be limited to a select few customers whose need for the good is of such a degree to warrant the price paid. Set the price too low, and the firm may not be able to attain long-term viability. All in all, the marketplace helps the business owner determine whether or not their solution to a marketplace is in fact the *job to be done* (Harvard Professor Clayton Christensen's term).

Charities do not have this same sort of mechanism. As long as the organization can continue to raise whatever funds are necessary to keep the doors open, they will continue to do so. If a competing theory of change provides a better, faster, cheaper answer to solving the issue, there is not necessarily an incentive for the existing nonprofit to change tactics to the alternative vision. This is doubly true when you have boards of directors involved, which often brings ego and social standing into the mix.

The second challenge philanthropy faces is in fact the same issue that Hippocrates raised when drafting his oath for physicians—do no harm. Far too often, in providing aid to others, a given theory of change involves a community outsider arriving with a greater pool of financial resources and an assumed superiority. When that happens, the potential for negative effects are in fact limitless.

Those who are receiving aid could in fact become entirely dependent on it. Moreover, the solutions developed and presented could be suboptimal if they're developed in isolation from the communities they're seeking to serve. As such, the solution provided may fit as comfortably in a community as a new woolen Christmas sweater given to an eight-year-old.

The Philanthropic Tide Is Shifting to Results

Because of these concerns and the leadership of many of the top charities, results have become a major focus. Philanthropic activity in the aggregate has seen massive growth since the 1980s, increasing from $145 billion in 1981 to an estimated $390 billion in 2016, even after adjusting for inflation.

Taking into account the estimated levels of wealth transfer anticipated over the coming decades, there are sizable amounts of funds that will likely be directed to charities. As the baby boomers continue to age, an unprecedented transfer of wealth is occurring as the assets of the boomers are passed on to the next-largest demographic cohort, the millennials. Paul Schervish and John Havens at the Boston College Center for Wealth and Philanthropy estimate that $59 trillion in wealth will be passed to future generations by the year 2061.

The days of *spray-pray-walk-away* philanthropy are ending, as individuals find that it's often not aligned with their most heartfelt passions and, as a result, they do not find the level of fulfillment they hoped for. People are shifting from supporting a broad variety of causes to a few that they're passionate about.

As givers make that shift, alongside a personal philanthropic vision and core values, the next step is to understand what type of giving is most appealing. Just as we have different personalities, we having giving styles that are a reflection of who we are and the change we want to see in the world. For example, understanding whether you like philanthropy that takes big risks to bring a new idea to fruition or that you prefer to support systemic changes. Each approach will be reflected in the types of organizations and projects you ultimately would like to fund.

There is a host of academic research being conducted about how this next generation will change their philanthropic approach versus prior generations. This philanthropic impulse is being further manifested in the use of socially responsible and environmentally sustainable approaches to investment as well, where profit-seeking capital is used to support causes or avoid things like fossil fuels.

This next generation wants to materially move the needle on the causes they're passionate about. They are much more willing to take risk and they want to see sizable impact. As a generation, 75 percent were volunteering before the age of fifteen. See Goldseker and Moody's excellent book *Generation Impact: How Next Gen Donors Are Revolutionizing Giving*. There is a desire to roll up their sleeves and contribute talents in addition to treasure. In fact, they believe their talents and networks can create more of an impact than the dollars alone. For women philanthropists, one interesting trend highlighted was the rise of giving collectives or giving circles as a way for women to partner together in stewarding their philanthropic dollars.

Philanthropy continues to grow in importance. Efforts like The Giving Pledge, a public declaration to give away at least 50 percent of financial assets, have raised the public profile of many billionaires who will be giving away sizable sums over the coming years. Yet as *The Atlantic* magazine noted after the death of Paul Allen, one of the multi-billionaire Microsoft founders, giving away a billion dollars may sound easy in theory, but it's much more difficult to do in actuality.

No doubt we've just scratched the surface of this topic, but regardless of your level of wealth, these are important considerations to ponder as you allocate your charitable resources.

Books to Consider

The Billionaire Who Wasn't: How Chuck Feeney Secretly Made and Gave Away a Fortune, Conor O'Clery

How to Change the World: Social Entrepreneurs and the Power of New Ideas, David Bornstein

Give Smart: Philanthropy That Gets Results, Thomas J. Tierney and Joel L. Fleishman

When Helping Hurts: How to Alleviate Poverty without Hurting the Poor—and Yourself, Steve Corbett and Brian Fikkert

God and Money: How We Discovered True Riches at Harvard Business School, John Cortines and Gregory Baumer

Generation Impact: How Next Gen Donors Are Revolutionizing Giving. Sharna Goldseker and Michael Moody. Hoboken: Wiley. 2017.

Gospels of Wealth: How the Rich Portray Their Live, Paul G. Schervish, Platon E. Coutsoukis, and Ethan Lewis

Wealth and the Will of God: Discerning the Use of Riches in the Service of Ultimate Purpose, Paul G. Schervish and Keith Whitaker

CHAPTER 12

BUILDING A LIFE OF INTENTION

"The unexamined life is not worth living."

—SOCRATES

---

hus far, we've explored deeply and carefully the nature of wealth, the positive choices we can make regarding it, and the constraints that shape our view of it. We have considered the structural elements of wealth—the wealth itself, our psychology, and how we came into wealth. We next shifted to the components of wealth identity and how our view of self, combined with core statements of purpose, vision, and values serve as powerful North Stars for our decision-making regarding wealth. Finally, we considered how these pieces integrate through the four pathways of what we do with wealth—spend, invest, bequeath, and give.

Now consider how these components are all brought together to create an articulated wealth strategy, how that strategy is monitored over time, and how it's updated when necessary. As I outline the case for your need to develop a wealth strategy, I'm assuming that you're one of the majority of people who don't have one. That's because in my experience, I've found this to be true. This observation is echoed by others who serve as professional advisors to the wealthy.

Let's consider the hypothetical case study of Mr. And Mrs. Smith. Although the Smiths are fictional, the scenario described is all too common. Mr. Smith spent thirty-five years building a local wallboard-distribution business. As the city grew and changed, Smith Wallboard was there to supply local contractors with the supplies they needed to literally build the future. Yet as he approached his sixty-fifth birthday, the phone rang and he received an offer from a private equity firm rolling up independent distributors all across the country. After working closely with his trusted advisors—probably his lawyer, his accountant, pastor, and wife—he decided to explore the offer for his business and move closer to a sale.

What can we assume about Mr. Smith? In my experience, successful entrepreneurs are not necessarily highly strategic by nature. Strategy implies a systematic and conscious way of reaching a solution to a problem. Entrepreneurs generally find themselves addressing problems that are not structured well enough for a systematic solution to make sense. By their very nature, entrepreneurs are used to high levels of ambiguity, and the way they respond to uncertainty is to find ways to make small bets that can fail quickly, thereby showing them the likely cleanest path forward through the fog.

So when Mr. and Mrs. Smith arrive on the private equity firm's doorstep, they have landed in a new world. In addition to a new world, there is both an entirely new language to learn and an almost daunting range of choices. Suddenly, many of the existing structures of life before the deal have been wiped away.

Not only must the couple begin to deal with the emotional consequences of monetizing a life's work; they must also begin to articulate aspirations for the future. Yet in the vast majority of cases when I've asked a client to talk about their goals/ priorities, it's as if this question had never been pondered before. And truly for most folks, money in life is a bit like a stream. It flows into a bank account with the paycheck, flows out with the credit card bill. Whatever is left behind is available for investment.

As a result, it can be hard to distill priority from action because much of how money is deployed is reactive in nature or done in a split-second decision—other than perhaps the most significant of life's expenditures, such as buying a house or car. But even then, I am regularly surprised by those who go out on a sunny Saturday afternoon and return home having bought a new car, when they meant to just run to the corner store to grab a newspaper.

An autopsy of past spending choices through credit card statements, tax returns, and charitable receipts can help uncover latent priorities. But such a deductive approach is hardly robust enough to set larger goals by. So at the risk of everything I've said so far being a large disclaimer, it's important to acknowledge that implementing the steps in this book requires a shift in mindset and a change in behavior. And let's be honest, none of us really likes change.

Can People Change?

So knowing that change may be required, it's worthwhile to consider whether humans are in fact capable of it. Maybe I'm just a naïve optimist, but I would argue that yes humans can change, but it's not easy. We all seem to possess a degree of inertia that thwarts our own desires to change. I've seen in my friends and family's lives that this inertia can vary in huge ranges. Some are ready to leave a job that's not working out in an almost foolhardy fashion. Others may take years of sitting and waiting before they decide to make a change.

So what is going on here and what can we take away from this? First, I would point us to the writings of professor, author, and philosopher James K. A. Smith. Smith, in his book *You Are What You Love*, highlights a fundamental flaw of the modern world. As Smith explains, modernity assumes that a person ultimately is no more than a brain on a stick. At a functional level, we're just a thinking thing. So from this understanding of humanity, to change a human, we just need to change the thinking.

And we can see how this subtle mentality pervades our society. Whether it's religious groups, nonprofits, educational institutions, or even businesses, society spends an inordinate amount of money each year on training, development, and continuing education to change the mind—and therefore change the behavior.

Yet, using the failure rate of New Year's resolutions as a quick guide, we would all quickly agree that these change efforts are most often unsuccessful. We need a different approach to implement. To consider a different approach, I would highlight the work of a few different parties.

First let's consider the *immunity to change* framework. Robert Kegan, a professor at Harvard, has written a number of different books looking at how humans change. Moreover and perhaps more important, he helps run a consulting firm that works with executives to change how management works. Kegan distinguishes between two types of change—adaptive and tactical. Tactical changes are about knowledge. A coach instructing a basketball player about the right technique to shoot a free throw is working to refine technique around a fairly defined set of physics principles at work to ensure the arc of the ball's flight delivers it through the hoop.

This is a fundamentally different type of change from an executive who is working to be more successful at delegating to subordinates. Adaptive changes require a deeper level of change in order to be implemented. There is more at work than just simple knowledge. This response to adaptive change forms the core of what Kegan refers to as *immunity to change.*

Earlier I referred to change as overcoming a moment of inertia, as if we are like a brick sitting on a table waiting to be pushed with enough force to move. Kegan would argue that in fact there is a lot of force being exerted to make change happen—both in attempting and implementing the new change. But in the same way that every action requires an equal and opposite reaction, Kegan points out there is a countervailing force working against the desired change.

What Kegan outlines then is a process by which an individual can explore the "competing commitments" that are hindering a person from implementing a change. Only once those hidden elements are revealed and can be acknowledged and determined to be true or not can a person be successful in implementing change. A quick Google search will lead you to Kegan's *Harvard Business Review* article "The Real Reason People Won't Change". Take ten minutes to read it sometime. Once we understand that we're more than just thinking things and that there are competing forces at work, it's helpful to consider what emerging psychological research shows about how people change.

Dan and Chip Heath's *Switch: How to Change When Change Is Hard* offers a number of excellent pointers along those lines. One of their key messages is the power of habits in influencing change. Habits allow us to navigate our lives and minimize the cognitive load required to get through our days. As such, they are immensely powerful. Once we start something and it becomes habitual, it's extremely challenging to undo it. Ramit Sethi, the author of *I Will Teach You to Be Rich,* is quick to highlight the power of microhabits.

Rather than trying to go full steam ahead and implement the entire desired change, start extremely small. If you want to start flossing your teeth, your goal is not to floss every tooth, every night. Instead, aim to floss only one tooth. That commitment is so innocuous and small that generally everyone can agree that they have the time in their schedule to floss a single tooth. Of course, once you have done a single one, you're likely to do others.

Charles Duhigg's great book *The Power of Habit* looks at how the cycle of cues, routines, and rewards subconsciously underlie a meaningful portion of the things we do each day. Knowing that, by understanding our cues, we can work to avoid existing habits we wish to replace, or perhaps more powerfully, rewire the cues to build new routines.

These three concepts of competing commitments, microhabits, and cues are important psychological tools we can use. But let's take all this analysis and outline a framework for what to do next. In discussing this framework, I do so being fully aware of the change in mentality required to think this way and the change in behavior needed to align your actions with your own strategic plan.

At davidcwellsjr.com/book, you'll find a template of the tool we've built to construct a strategic wealth plan. The three parts align with the three parts of this book: structure, identity, and strategy.

Wealth Structure

The tool begins with analyzing the elements of wealth structure. The first tab is a place to compile a whole-life balance sheet. A balance sheet is typically used in organizations to show the assets (things that are used to create value) in comparison to the liabilities. Families may have a financial balance sheet compiled, but one that is highly incomplete. Instead, the goal is to put together a complete balance sheet that lists the human assets, intellectual assets, and social relationships alongside a complete financial picture. Arguably, without the other elements, the financial picture does not fully communicate all the resources you have available at your disposal to bring to bear on a particular problem or goal.

In the same way, it expands the notion of liability to consider deficits in each of the categories. This would include poor personal relationships, skill/learning gaps relative to what you want to achieve in your life, as well as having the meaningful personal connections that are so critical to human flourishing.

Secondly, the tool offers a place to consider the key aspects of psychology that may be currently affecting how we think about our wealth. As well, knowing how important it is to deeply understand the source of ones wealth, and the accompanying implications, there is a place to respond to that as well.

Wealth Identity

Next the tool walks through the Self-and-Money Framework from Chapter 6. There is a series of four questions designed to help you understand how your *self* and *wealth* are in relationship. It is important to highlight that such an exercise may raise a number of serious questions and concerns that are best walked through with a trained counselor. There are many wealth-focused counselors who have specific background in helping the wealthy make peace with the issues that surround wealth in their lives and which may be having a negative impact.

Next, the tool walks you through the key steps to articulating purpose, values, and vision. Just as any trip to the doctor begins with diagnosis, this portion of the tool begins in a similar way.

The first set of questions is about diving deeply into what is most important for you:

1. If you woke up with so much money that having enough was no longer a concern and you had less

than ten years to live, what would you start and stop doing in your life?

2. If your eulogy were delivered today, what would it say about you and what should it say about you?

3. What are your regular, consistent worries and fears?

I've adapted these questions from a couple of different sources, so I do not claim that they're unique. Nevertheless, they are effective in helping to focus your attention on what your real priorities are for your life, along with what in life may be holding you back from reaching them.

Building on this foundation, the process shifts to examining the past twelve months. The Paterson Center and its founder Tom Paterson outline in their work four questions to consider: What is working well? What is not working and should be changed? What is confusing? And what is missing? I consider those questions across each of life's five major dimensions—self, marriage, family, work, and community.

These questions are highly comprehensive and allow the right mix of celebration and critique. *What is working well?* is a question that surfaces your wins. It's important to observe and make a record of your successes. After a tough stretch, it's often easy to forget the great things that have happened. There is a saying that we overestimate how much we can do in a short period of time and underestimate how much we can accomplish over a much longer period. With that sentiment, the chance to log and reflect is a great calibration tool as you later begin to consider your bigger goals for the year ahead.

Paterson's questions look to uncover a thing that can be improved but do so across three different dimensions. The first question—*What is not working and should be changed?*—is excellent at surfacing the things that clearly need to go. No doubt, we all have things in life that we're holding on to at any given period of time that need to be moved aside.

In the same vein, consider *What are things that I'm doing right now that are holding me back from achieving my goals?* This may be a great opportunity to go to your boss and/or personal mentors to solicit some honest and candid feedback. What will I do differently? What are things that I am doing but with some refinement and improvement will be much more effective in driving me to accomplish my goals?

Paterson's next two questions are genius in that they tease out things that may not blatantly be working today but could lead to your goal over time. He asks *What's confusing?* and *What's missing?*

Things that are confusing may not surface as front-burner problems, but in my experience, they're correlated with the issue that surfaces over time. By digging into them early, we can find those things that are controllable—issues that are fixable with the right corrective action, personal development, relationships etc. For those that are not fixable, it may be that they are surfacing one of life's paradoxes (also known as a polarity).

Understanding the nature of paradox (and how it differs from a problem) is vitally important. A problem has a clear, singular answer for a solution. If your car is broken down, the solution to the problem is to take it to a mechanic. A paradox is something different. Paradoxes are scenarios where both sides are true at the same time. As F. Scott Fitzgerald noted, "The test of a first-rate intelligence is the ability to hold two opposing ideas in mind at the same time and still retain the ability to function." Although that may be true for a first-rate intelligence, we all ultimately prefer the simplicity of a singular idea that is true.

A common paradox in life is the desire for change versus the desire for stability. We all likely have a preference between the two that's informed by our own personal background and characteristics. Nevertheless, organizations that persist for a long time find some way to preserve the essentials of the organization, and find ways to change and grow. Amazon started off its corporate life as a humble seller of books, an activity that continues to this day, alongside a whole host of other business ventures.

Likely in your life, as in mine, there are paradoxes, which are not solvable with a singular answer. Answering the question about what is confusing may likely surface some that are in your life. Understanding that these paradoxes are present is highly important to their management. Paterson's final question is *What is missing?* This is a life-planning version of the *clean-up* question that great interviewers ask: *What should I have asked that I did not?* Things that are missing may not actively be hindering life in the same way that a problem is, but they may be keeping life from reaching its greatest fulfillment.

Building a Life and Wealth Strategy

Using the diagnostic data you've generated, the next step is to translate that into a simplified life strategy. The key elements of that are a *why* statement (that is, a mission statement), core values, and then an articulation of your vision for self, family, work, and community.

The wealth strategy is the second step of the process that may be new to you. We discussed the four primary uses of financial wealth available to each of us—consumption, philanthropy, legacy, and investment. We discussed each of those in Chapters 9-12, but now the goal is to shift that broad knowledge into strategic choices, recognizing that each category is interrelated to the others

Defining a consumption strategy is about answering the question of where you draw an end-point for your standard of living. You may choose to outline specific consumption dreams around things you would like to own someday or experiences you would like to have. Nevertheless, as we discussed earlier, the satisfaction we derive from consumption is declining due to the phenomena of hedonic adaptation—the point being that we simply cannot consume our way to happiness. If that's the case, why not define a finish line and recognize that when you've reached it, there will have to be other things in your life to make up for any perceived lack of unhappiness.

Investing for the future is closely tied to the question of consumption. In the first stages of investment, it's about accumulating an adequate base of assets to support your consumption when you're unable or no longer desire to work to generate a means of living. Once that threshold has been crossed, you enter the second stage of investment, which is about funding the legacy and philanthropic priorities you have identified. Thinking about investment in those three buckets may be helpful. With your trusted advisor, you will likely need to dig into questions about the long-range return potential of assets, etc.

The final two categories of a wealth strategy are about how you intend to give your assets away. There is of course a fifth and final way to use your assets—to pay taxes—but I have yet to meet anyone who voluntarily is cutting additional checks to the government. For each of these categories, there are a tremendous number of questions worth considering in significant detail to ensure your desires and intentions are accurately reflected in your plans.

Implementation

The implementation phase is characterized by taking the strategic documents from the prior phase and translating them into a doable set of next steps. Since we all live life annually, I have designed the process to be conducted on that basis. Personally, this is something I engage in during the fourth quarter of every year.

Just as a business may go through a period of annual budgeting and planning, it's important that we conduct a similar exercise ourselves. A common sort of reflection people do is a list of New Year's resolutions. Diet companies, health clubs, and countless other business models are built on this natural inclination to do something different/better at the start of each year.

Yet I think we're all familiar with how poorly we perform in terms of keeping or realizing the fruits of our well-intentioned resolutions. At our core, it's hard to change habits, and we're all poor at deploying our limited self-will to implement change. Moreover, twelve months is an extremely long period of time, making it even more difficult to make the best choices today. After all, I can always go to the gym tomorrow, right?

If you've done the first steps correctly and come armed with the key inputs, you should be well prepared to begin thinking about the year ahead. Here is what we bring to this phase:

- ➔ personal mission statement
- ➔ personal values
- ➔ successes from last year—to build upon in the year ahead
- ➔ opportunities for improvement

Before I draft specific annual goals, I always draft a vision statement for the year ahead. In many cases, my vision for the year ahead is captured in a single word. For example, my vision for this year has been the word *clarity*.

Next, building off the major life dimensions from the life strategy, I work to build out goals for each of self, family, community, and work.

Self is a large enough category that I further segment into mind/body/soul goals to make sure that I encapsulate everything from personal development to physical health to fun to spiritual development. I even go so far as to plan goals around fun and enjoyment. I've found that unless I specify in advance how many rounds of golf I want to play in a year, I never seem to have the time to get the rounds in.

Family Goals. There are many moving pieces for what could be included under family goals. I narrow the scope to consider my vision for myself in the context of my marriage and family. Defining who I want to be as a husband and father, and understanding where I may be off from that has over time proven to be extremely valuable as I consider my own personal development. For your family overall, I would recommend engaging in a similar sort of strategy building and planning exercise with your spouse.

Community. Community includes everything from social relationships to the non-profit causes and organizations that you care most about in the world.

Work. Professional or work goals may be complex enough to warrant their own separate strategic plan to consider the various dimensions for success.

Metrics, the Forgotten Step

Once you've completed your specific goals by section, you have to specify what the metrics are for measurement. It could be a certain frequency for dates with your significant other, a specific number of books you want to read, or how frequently you want to work out. For each goal, put a metric beside it that allows this tracking. As you articulate the specific goals, it's of paramount importance to focus on process steps and not outcomes.

A few examples: If in the year ahead, I say that I want to be a good husband to my wife. This is a nebulous goal that's fairly difficult to determine. So I look at what being a good husband means for my wife. What does she value as being most important to her? Maybe this is spending a certain amount of time together each week or having regular date nights. These are the key inputs into the ultimate outcome and are much easier to target a specific goal around.

Professionally, the list could include any number of things. If you need to drive more revenue, work to determine what the precedent steps are for that. Do you need more new clients? Do you need to keep in touch with folks more regularly? This could lead to specific goals of making a targeted number of phone calls per day or aiming for a particular number of meetings per week, for example.

Set It and Forget It

Ron Popeil was correct with his Showtime Rotisserie Oven: "setting and forgetting" really is the easiest way. Drafting the goals is the first step, but to stay on track with your goals, you need to close the loop on all this by creating two recurring calendar invites.

First, schedule a monthly review. I typically schedule fifteen to twenty minutes late in the afternoon on the first Monday of each month. I use this time to compile my metrics data and log the results into my goal tracking spreadsheet. This does not have to be super time consuming For example, I want to work out at least three times a week. I keep an old school paper calendar at my office, where each day that I work out, I write an *E* on the calendar. During my review, I total up the *E*s and divide by four—giving me the frequency of how often I worked out that month.

Second, schedule a quarterly progress report. This may be more like thirty minutes to an hour. Schedule a calendar invite for once every three months on a Friday afternoon. With that time, review each category and the progress along each goal. You may add to your goals, remove, or mark them complete. These two recurring calendar invites set the predictability and repeatability necessary to keep you on the path toward achieving each year's goals.

Conclusion

The task of living strategically with wealth is fraught with challenges. As the title of this book intones, When Anything is Possible, knowing where to begin and how to proceed is daunting. The number of possible options and choices is breathtaking. As well, because we each come to wealth in our own way, knowing how to integrate the benefits and responsibilities of wealth can often times feel like navigating an alien land. As if that were not complicated enough, while there are a few hard and fast guidelines, most considerations regarding wealth are highly nuanced and dependent on circumstances. A number of years ago I was speaking to a group about thoughtful consumption. A younger woman asked me in the room a really specific question trying to get a to a hard and fast dollar figure answer to a question. And yet despite her desire for specifics, the only correct response was to walk her deeper in with additional questions. No doubt, for some, that can be infuriating, but that is the nature of wealth.

Throughout this book, I have attempted to walk you through a holistic way of thinking about your wealth and arm you with frameworks and tools to deploy it well. If I could leave you with a final piece of advice, it would be this: When in doubt, "go slow to go fast." That refrain is common among the Navy Seal community as they train and prepare for truly life-and-death missions. My understanding of its meaning is that when we rush to move things along, we oftentimes make mistakes that take even longer to recover from. Instead, proceeding slowly and deliberately will undoubtedly get us where we seek to go and most likely at exactly the right time. So when you encounter questions that you haven't contemplated before, do not be afraid to slow the process down, to pause. In that place of quiet, you can gather the necessary wisdom about yourself and seek the wise counsel of others needed to navigate to the other side. I wish you all the best as you travel the path ahead.

Books to Consider

• *Halftime: Moving From Success to Significance*, Bob Buford and Jim Collins

• *Living the Life You Were Meant to Live*, Tom Paterson

• *Essentialism: Do Less but Accomplish More, Guide to Identifying the Essential Things, Focus on and Getting Them Done*, Martin Hell

• *The 4-Hour Workweek: Escape 9-5, Live Anywhere, and Join the New Rich*, Timothy Ferriss

BONUS MATERIAL

Visit davidcwellsjr.com/book for a free download of the "When Anything is Possible" Worksheet

The worksheet has templates to complete all the steps discussed in this book.

ABOUT THE AUTHOR

As an Author, Strategist, and Advisor, David has been working closely with individuals, families and companies at the intersection of investment, strategy, and governance for the last 15 years. He is the Founder and CEO of Family Capital Strategy, a boutique consultancy that provides strategic insight, investment governance development and family office design for families facing liquidity events, generational transitions, and other significant changes.

Prior to founding the firm, David has an extensive background conducting strategic and investment analysis, having served as a Partner and Portfolio manager at a 20-year old asset management firm, co-founder of a long-short hedge fund, and a senior equity analyst working with large hedge fund and private equity clients.

David has and continues to serve in a broad range of governance roles. David is the Chairman of the Board and Chairman of the Investment Committee for the private trust company of a Midwestern family. As well, he currently serves as Chairman of the Board of Nashville Classical

Charter School, one of the top-performing schools in the state of Tennessee. He is also on the Board of 21/64, a national practice advising family philanthropies.

An Eagle Scout, David is a graduate of Wake Forest University, magna cum laude, Beta Gamma Sigma. He has completed executive education course work on Family Business Governance at Northwestern University's Kellogg School of Management. Additionally, he is a Chartered Financial Analyst (CFA) charter holder. He is also a 21/64 Certified Advisor for those who work in an advisory role with multi-generational families.

He was recognized in 2017 as one of Nashville's Forty under Forty and in 2019 as a recipient of a Nashville Emerging Leader Award – Financial Services Industry. In 2020, he was recognized by the Nashville Post as part of their All-Star Board.